The Journey of Grandparent Alienation & Estrangement

Carolyn Carter

Published by Carolyn Carter, 2024.

.

Table of Contents

This book is for parents and grandparents who find themselves on the heartbreaking journey of alienation and estrangement. Special thanks to those who shared their stories, personal experiences, and insights in an effort to offer peace and hope along the way.

Disclaimer: This book is not a professional therapy resource and is not intended to treat, diagnose, cure, or replace mental health professional care and/or medical treatment.

FOREWORD

———

Grandchildren are the crown of the aged.

PROVERBS 17:6 (ESV)

For many, being a grandparent is eagerly anticipated as one of the most special seasons of a person's life. GrandPARENTing is a time for snuggles, hugs, cookie making, sleepovers, storybook reading, family dinners, holiday celebrations, and faith nurturing. It's all about patience, love, acceptance, and encouragement. It's about connecting grandchildren to their heritage and sharing lots of "when I was your age" stories. As estranged grandPARENTS, it is difficult to find ourselves "dethroned" from our anticipated role and rejected by our adult children. Our hearts are aching, and we are filled with sadness. We are faced with the reality that the grandPARENTing road in our life is closed. We have been given no choice but to take a detour down a path that is very different from what we had envisioned. It is not the idyllic one we had planned for our family and certainly not the one we wanted to take. Instead, we find ourselves on a new journey—a journey to find peace, for now, and hope for the future in the midst of the very real hurt of family alienation and estrangement.

Trust in the Lord with all your heart, and lean not on your own understanding; In all your ways acknowledge Him, and He shall direct your paths.

PROVERBS 3:5-6 (ESV)

1

INTRODUCTION

———

Undelivered Message to My Son

I do not understand all that has happened in the last few years. I cannot tell you how hurtful it is to feel rejected by a son, rebuked by a daughter-in-law, and disconnected from my grandchildren. I remember your birth many years ago and all the joy you brought into my life, more joy with your marriage, and even more joy upon the birth of your children, my grandchildren—the best thing in the world! I hope your precious children know that my love for them has not ended. I hope that one day your newborn will know she has a grandmother who loves her. I hope and pray you will never experience the heartache of estrangement.

My Story

Upon the end of my teaching career, I spent a number of years caring for my grandchildren while their parents, my son and daughter-in-law, worked their daily jobs. I was happy to be able to help, as I felt it was a way to give back to my son. Full-time teaching and parenting had presented its challenges in finding enough time in his childhood to devote to each responsibility. I enjoyed spending time with my grandchildren, and I developed a close, loving relationship with each one.

Then, one day, the unthinkable happened. I was declared an overbearing mother-in-law and told that, going forward, my child care services were no longer needed. I was to keep my distance and stay out of their lives. All of these bewildering and distressing statements were communicated via the impersonal avenue of text messaging. Needless to say, the dreams of my happy golden years had been shattered and replaced with nothing but sadness and heartache.

My Journey

The onset of my family's estrangement brought more hurt than I could ever imagine. It was not an acceptable situation, and I was determined to fix my broken family! After crying out to God in despair, I sprang into action. I talked with a few close friends to seek advice. I read book after book after book seeking to understand the reason for the rejection by my son and daughter-in-law to uncover a path forward to renew our relationship. I reached out to them and made every effort to reconcile in the best way I knew how. After a couple years of attempting to repair my broken family, I had made little progress. I was still a very sad, estranged mother and grandmother. I was overwhelmed, and I needed help.

I finally recognized that I could not successfully repair my broken family on my own. Even though I prayed daily, I realized that I needed to give the whole set of circumstances up to God and more fully rely on him for strength and guidance. That would require that I give up my desire for control and focus less on my own attempts to resolve the situation. The problem was just too big for me to work out. I remember feeling such a sense of relief when I finally turned all my troubles over to God. And then God placed this Bible verse on my heart as a reminder: "Trust in the Lord with all your heart, and do not lean on your own understanding" (Proverbs 3:5 ESV).

Trust in the Lord. Now, that was the hard part. Was God really there? Was God in the midst of all my hurt? I sure felt like I was all alone and that God didn't care. But Scripture reminded me that God had not left my side and had even provided me with a "forever helper." The evidence of this is found in the words of John 14:18 (ESV) which state that before Jesus left this world, he announced he would not leave us as orphans. He said, "I will ask the Father, and he will give you another Helper to be with you forever" (John 14:16 ESV). How comforting it was to be reminded that the Helper God promised is the Holy Spirit who lives *with* us and *in* us (John 14:17 ESV).

Despite those reassuring words, I wondered how I would even sense the presence of the Holy Spirit, especially when my life's journey had become such a bumpy road, and God seemed so distant. Knowing that the Holy Spirit communicates predominantly through the written words of Scripture, I searched for answers. In my readings I uncovered countless words of wisdom and guidance regarding burdens, negative emotions, relationships, forgiveness, reconciliation, hope, and much more. The Holy Spirit, through the words of Scripture, did indeed provide me with direction as I pondered how to respond to ongoing disparaging text messages from my daughter-in-law, deliberated the prudence of reaching out one more time to initiate reconciliation, and considered how God would want me to respond to these hurtful circumstances in my life. An interesting side note is that while reviewing the research for this book on some of the above topics, I was absolutely amazed at how many times scientific studies backed up and supported Scripture! God's Word is most certainly true.

The Bible points to other ways in which the Holy Spirit communicates. For example, when Nehemiah expressed his desire to rebuild the walls of Jerusalem, he said it was because of "what my God had put into my heart to do" (Nehemiah 2:12 ESV). When Paul was in Athens he spoke of his spirit being provoked within him (Acts 17:16). Our thoughts and those feelings of gentle nudges within us may very well be the "voice" of the Holy Spirit leading and guiding us.

Sure enough, near the end of the two-year mark of my estrangement, I felt a nudge, a tug on my heart from the Holy Spirit to begin a support group at my church. I resisted this "little push" from God at first. After all, my calling in life was to be a teacher. I had no experience as a support group leader, and the very thought of becoming involved in care ministries was way out of my comfort zone. Eventually, I realized I could not walk away from this project God had placed on my heart. Fortunately, the knowledge gained from the books I studied provided discussion topics for our newly formed care ministry. In addition, God blessed this endeavor with an experienced and technologically talented co-facilitator who became my mentor. The grandPARENTS in attendance shared their stories and their feelings of sadness and hopelessness. (Note: The information in this book is pertinent to grandparents, as well as to parents who do not yet have grandchildren.) We worked through the concepts of forgiveness, explored avenues for reconciliation, and focused on the process of healing. All of this resulted in the writing and production of a faith-based workbook for estranged grandPARENTS. Due to the interest expressed, it soon became apparent that hurting grandparents from across the country were seeking guidance and support and that one church could not meet the needs of all. The inspiration for this book was born. Hopefully alienated grandPARENTS from many geographical areas will be blessed by the faith-based contents of this book.

Parents and grandparents are encouraged to read this book individually or together in small groups with others who are on the same journey of family alienation and estrangement. Whether the groups are formed as book clubs, support groups, or care ministries, connecting with other believers in Christ provides opportunities to strengthen all those involved. Sharing our stories of family estrangement, as well as the heartaches and other negative emotions experienced, helps lighten burdens and mitigate hurt. God's Word found in Galatians 6:2 (ESV) specifically encourages us to "bear one another's burdens" and in 2 Corinthians 1:4 (NIV) "to comfort those in any trouble with the comfort we ourselves receive from God." Discourse on topics such as negative emotions, forgiveness, reconciliation, boundaries, relationships, acceptance, gratitude, staying present, and family dynamics, open the door to talking through concerns that are specific to estranged families. A conversation roadmap for facilitating discussion is included at the end of the book. It is hoped that each reader and small group will find peace for the present, hope for the future, and come to know they are not alone on this journey!

Weathering the Storms of Life

―――

You rule the raging of the sea; when its waves rise, you still them.

Psalm 89:9 ESV

Thunderstorms occur regularly in many states and often cause serious property damage to roofs, windows, siding, gutters, and vehicles. According to the National Weather Service, approximately 100,000 storms sweep over the United States per year. Based on information from the Insurance Information Institute, around $950 million in property damage occurred in 2022 alone. Devastated homeowners face the task of assessing the damage, gathering insurance quotes, and hiring contractors to complete the repairs.

In the event of physical destruction to property, procedures for restoration have been established, and solutions are possible. But, in the event that a family becomes shattered due to broken relationships, the course of action is often unclear and unsettling. Measures to restore the devastation caused by the emotional and spiritual storms of broken family relationships are not as easily discernible and straightforward.

Our first reaction may be one of disbelief, followed by ongoing and troublesome thoughts of this tragic storm in our life. No doubt, our unsettled feelings of despair will lead us to a never-ending search for peace. Rather than keep our feelings secret and bottled up inside, we may attempt to mitigate our sadness by sharing our story with others. In a state of bewilderment, we try to comprehend the "why," and we desperately long for the storm to pass.

We may question where God is in all of this and wonder how he could let these heartbreaking situations happen. Recall, in the very beginning of human existence, life *was* perfect and harmonious. The book of Genesis recounts the narrative of how God created the world and everything in it. God beheld that it was very good and beautiful! But in the Garden of Eden, sin entered the world, and sin brought with it a multitude of problems. Jesus reminds us that "in the world you will have tribulation" (John 16:33 ESV). Ever since sin entered our lives, humans can expect to endure suffering. We can be certain that our journey through life will be a bumpy road filled with numerous ups and downs. There will be summer, and there will be winter; there will be rainbows, and there will be storms. But Jesus reassures us that he will be with us always, even to the end of the age (Matthew 28:20 ESV). We can be reassured that Jesus will provide support, strength, and hope for us along the way.

How comforting to know that we can seek shelter from the storms of family estrangement in the arms of our Almighty God in whom we can place our trust and find respite. The Bible tells us not to fear and not to be dismayed for God is our God. In fact, the concept of "do not fear" appears in the Bible 365 times, one for each day of the year! Ask God to calm the storms in your life and give you a sense of peace for the present and hope for the future.

Great is our Lord, and abundant in power; His understanding is beyond measure.

(Psalm 147:5 ESV)

Phenomenon of Grandparent Alienation

Parent and grandparent alienation causes profoundly deep hurt. The situation can come on abruptly for no apparent reason, or it can develop over a period of time. Surely, estrangement causes emotional harm for grandparents, as well as children and grandchildren. Many grandparents have spent a lifetime nurturing a beautiful family. They are devastated and heartbroken when rejected by their adult children, and when they see their family crumbling right before their eyes. Grandchildren who have already formed a relationship with their grandparents become confused and wonder if they will ever see their grandparents again. Sadly, some grandparents have never been given the opportunity to meet their grandchildren.

Communication may be nonexistent or extremely stressful as a result of the estrangement. Grandparents feel as if they need to walk on eggshells to prevent the matter from getting worse. They may be on the receiving end of false accusations, unwelcome messages, and verbal abuse. Parents and grandparents are often at a loss as to which avenues, if any, to pursue in communicating with their adult children.

Estrangement begs one to question what happened to the concept of "family." It is a given that grandparents need grandchildren, and grandchildren need grandparents. In my contact with hurting grandparents, the phrase "I don't understand" is one that I have heard many times. Bewilderment describes the state of many alienated parents and grandparents. Family estrangement is indeed a sad and complex issue.

The "Why"

Discovering the "why" will not change our estrangement situation, but exploring possible causes may help us name the problem, identify what we need to forgive, and lift the burden of guilt off our own shoulders. Moreover, we may gain an understanding of the direction we need to take for reconciliation, and we may even find a reason for compassion. Following are some thoughts on the possible causes of grandparent alienation.

Silent Epidemic

Dr. Joshua Coleman, leading expert, psychologist, and author of *Rules of Estrangement: Why Adult Children Cut Ties & How to Heal the Conflict,* shares his thoughts on the matter. Coleman writes, "Labeled a silent epidemic by a growing number of therapists and researchers, estrangement is one of the most disorienting and painful experiences of a parent's life. Due to rising rates of individualism, an increasing cultural emphasis on happiness, growing economic insecurity, and a historically recent perception that parents are obstacles to personal growth, many parents find themselves forever shut out of the lives of their adult children and grandchildren [1]." Dr. Coleman's analysis certainly leads us to the understanding that we are not alone!

Change in Family Values

Parents and grandparents grew up in the times of "honor thy father and mother" and strong family units. One study [2] determined that grandparents tend to hold "normative assumptions about the permanence of parent-child relationships," as they believe family relationships are non-voluntary and forever. Conversely, if adult children believe or perceive their parents are harming their well-being, they are not obligated to remain in a relationship. Their emotional health seems to take precedence over loyalty to their family. It is interesting to note, according to another study [3], that adult children feel disagreements about politics and parenting are also grounds for alienation.

The realization of these changing times and resulting transformation in family values became apparent to me when my daughter-in-law sent a text message reprimanding me for assuming we would spend holidays together. The thought of not spending time with family over the holidays had never even occurred to me. Unbelievably, that very scenario was the expectation of my daughter-in-law.

We may begin to wonder if our adult children, who might not value family as much as we do, realize how much their rejection has hurt us. Consider the words uttered by Jesus as he hung on the cross: "Father, forgive them, for they know not what they do" (Luke 23:34 ESV). As Jesus is dying, he is forgiving the people who crucified him because they might not realize what they are doing! Likewise, is it possible that our adult children really do not know the pain they are causing us? Are they too busy with their lives to realize the depth of our heartache as we suffer the loss of what every parent and grandparent hopes for, the respect of their adult children and the opportunity to continue loving and caring for them and their family?

Influential Adversaries

In one study [4], 80 percent of grandparents stated they believed that an ex-husband, son-in-law, or daughter-in-law had turned their children against them. After leading several support groups for estranged grandparents, influential adversaries do indeed appear to be a significant contributing factor to alienation. Parents have difficulty understanding how the close relationship with their adult child could be undermined by the manipulative behavior of a son-in-law or daughter-in-law. Personally, I can relate. When my daughter-in-law defined me as an overbearing mother-in-law, my journey of alienation from my son and grandchildren began. I was hurt by the label "overbearing" and did not understand what led to this designation. My son was given the ultimatum to choose his wife or me. Because he did not want me to know what was happening in his marriage, and because he wanted to keep the peace in his family of three children, my son joined in the hurtful communication. It was difficult to lose the beloved son I had raised due to the hurtful actions of his wife. In addition, I felt betrayed by my daughter-in-law due to the fact that we had accepted her into our family over the years and loved her as well.

Mental Health Concerns

In the same study [5] as above, grandparents stated that their children's mental illness, including anxiety, depression, addiction, or alcoholism, played a role. If a loved one of yours has a diagnosed mental health condition or known addiction problem, it may be helpful to gain an understanding of some of their triggers and behaviors, as well as an explanation as to why individuals in those circumstances seem to react so differently than individuals not carrying those particular burdens. Dr. Joshua Coleman states that "from the perspective of the adult child, estrangement is every bit as necessary to their psychological survival and well-being as reconciliation is to the parent" [6, p. 235]. Professional therapists may be able to offer some valuable insights.

Unknown Causes

The onset of alienation often generates a sense of puzzlement among many grandparents. We are often left in a state of confusion as we try to determine the basis for such hurtful actions by our adult children. In the 2015 study by Carr [7],grandparents reported being unsure of the reason for their estrangement. It is interesting to note that in this study, adult children commonly blamed parents for being unsupportive and unaccepting. That finding creates more questions, and answers may be hard to come by if communication channels are strained.

Stories of Alienation and Estrangement

Everyone loves to hear a good story, especially one with a happy ending or a humorous outcome. However, there *are* benefits to taking in a sad movie or reading a heartbreaking book on occasion. Taking in these less-than-uplifting experiences may not be enjoyable, but exposure to the negative emotions of the characters can generate feelings of empathy and help us process our own hurt when sorrows come our way.

As a matter of fact, if you have a very sad, heartbreaking story to tell, sharing it can begin the process of healing.

Upon the realization that I had become an alienated grandmother, it was very difficult for me to keep all of the negative emotions associated with rejection to myself. I am forever grateful for dear friends and family members who listened empathetically to my story and offered their compassion. Telling my story helped me work through difficult emotions and begin to make sense of all that had happened.

Once again the words of the Bible ring true as the Apostle Paul advises the Galatians, "Bear one another's burdens, and so fulfil the law of Christ" (Galatians 6:2 ESV). We are tasked by God to be good listeners, to lighten the heavy load others are carrying, and to strengthen them. We usually want to be the "listener" and help someone else with their troubles. But there are times we need to be the "storyteller" and allow someone else to lighten *our* burdens.

As the following stories unfold, one can get a sense of the phenomenon of grandparent alienation and estrangement and the heavy loads many are carrying.

"My husband and I are not welcome to visit my son anymore. Only his brother and my father are allowed, and even those relationships have become of lesser value to my son as well."—Kaye

"I was deemed an overbearing mother-in-law."—Pat

"My husband and I have a controlling, jealous son-in-law creating drama. When we would ask our daughter to visit, she was thrilled, but less and less so over time. Our son-in-law is a pastor, which makes it worse."—Ann

"I am a wife and mother of three adult children, one of whom is married and has blessed my husband and me with two beloved grandchildren. After retiring I spent a few years caring for our grandchildren while our

son and daughter-in-law worked their daily jobs. Upon the birth of our third grandchild, my daughter-in-law planned to stay at home. At that point I was viewed as an unsupportive, manipulative mother-in-law and was not allowed to see my grandchildren any more. The sudden and unexpected loss of my family was overwhelming!"—Carolyn

Each quote above, as well as stories shared with me by other estranged grandparents, is different, but they share many commonalities. Many estranged grandparents have been unreasonably rejected by their adult children and denied ongoing familial relationships with them and their children. Many also reported feeling alone. During the first two years of my estrangement, I did not meet or become aware of any other grandparent in my situation. Finally, I came across some books on the topics of alienation and estrangement. Although I was sad to learn that many others are traveling the same road, I felt comfort in learning that I was not the only one on this difficult path!

We do not need to travel this journey alone. God has tasked us to "encourage one another and build one another up" (1 Thessalonians 5:11 ESV). We can connect with friends, other family members, relatives, pastors, counselors, and therapists in an effort to strengthen one another. We can pray for each other, and we can ask God to bless us with his peace, heal our aching hearts, and provide us with guidance.

The Lord is close to the brokenhearted; He rescues those who are crushed in spirit.

(Psalm 34:18 ESV)

What's Your Story?

Grandparent alienation causes flurries of emotions to swirl around in our minds. Those negative feelings may even consume and control our lives. We may find ourselves living in a constant state of sadness, hopelessness, and heartache. We may find it difficult to think rationally. We can begin the process of healing by thinking about our situation and then finding the words to write *our* stories. Journaling helps one define and name a troubling circumstance in life and provides a stepping stone to move forward.

For those of you who love journaling, you may be grateful for the opportunity to put your story into words. You may find that you fill page after page with your thoughts and reflections. But if the word "journaling" causes you angst, consider the option of writing just a few sentences to express your story. No matter your level of enthusiasm for the writing process, remember that the main goal is to identify and define your situation.

Share Your Story

According to Galatians 6:5 (ESV), "each will have to bear his own *load*." That is, each one should be responsible for their daily tasks in life and not expect others to complete them. In contrast, Galatians 6:2 (ESV) calls us to "bear one another's *burdens*." The term "burden" refers to a difficulty so great that one cannot bear it alone. Certainly the weight of grandparent estrangement can be categorized as a burden to be shared with others.

You may be wondering how you could possibly reveal your story to anyone. Others may think you did something wrong to cause the alienation. The fear of feeling judged may cause you to hesitate. You may feel ashamed and embarrassed. You may not want to tell someone that your loving family is now a broken family.

There is no denying that the above concerns are real. I personally experienced them all at the onset of my alienation. Eventually, I did muster enough courage to tell my story because the hurt became too much to bear on my own. I shared my family situation with a dear friend and also a next-door neighbor. Their willingness to listen, their empathy, and their sorrow meant the world to me. It did indeed help me through a difficult time. When you feel comfortable, choose someone to help you carry the pain and lighten your burdens.

Thoughts about Suffering

We hope our journey through life will be one filled with sunshine, clear skies, roses, happiness, and lots of smiles. But Jesus' very words, "in this world you *will* have trouble," caution us that this will not be the case. Unfortunately, that means there is a 100% chance our life will include problems of some kind. We may encounter illness, financial setbacks, sadness, job loss, or broken family relationships along the way. However, Jesus reassures us with these words: "take heart, I have overcome the world" (John 16:33 ESV).

What did Jesus mean when he said that he has overcome the world? It points to the fact that Jesus has conquered sin and death and that we can place our hope in him, our almighty and powerful God. We do not have to rely on our own abilities. Trusting in Jesus to answer our prayers in his way and in his timing can bring the peace we are seeking.

The Bible also provides some compelling thoughts about suffering:

We rejoice in our sufferings, knowing that suffering produces endurance, and endurance produces character, and character produces hope, and hope does not put us to shame, because God's love has been poured into our hearts through the Holy Spirit who has been given to us.

(Romans 5:3-7 ESV)

Seriously? Rejoice in our sufferings? Take note that Paul, the author of the book of Romans, did not say to rejoice for our sufferings. Rather, we are to rejoice in our sufferings, in the midst of our trials. When troubles come our way, we most certainly should acknowledge the pain, the hurt, the fear, the heartache, and the sadness. We are allowed to cry out to God. We do not have to put on a happy face and pretend our negative emotions do not exist. However, we can also recognize that suffering is not in vain as it produces endurance, and endurance produces character, and character produces hope. In what do we put our hope? We put our hope in Jesus. Placing our hope in other people, who may let us down, is not sensible or wise. Placing our hope in the things of this world will let us down. But if we put our hope in Jesus, suffering will not have the final say. Suffering will not be the end of the story.

The Journey of Estrangement

You may feel that you are experiencing the saddest, most heartbreaking time in your life. Grief and hopelessness fill your days. You are rejected, and you miss your adult children and beloved grandchildren. You are thrown off balance and wonder how life could have taken such a turn. You feel your life will end this way and that your happy golden years are an unrealizable dream. It is a journey you never expected to take. Where do you start? The answer is to start right where you are. Then, turn to God for direction and guidance and know that he is listening.

Give yourself time to work through all that has happened. The process of healing will require patience. Perhaps there are steps in the future you will be able to take toward reconciliation, and your estrangement situation will be resolved. That would be wonderful! Or perhaps you will come to the realization that the situation is out of your control, for now, and you need to work on getting your life out of the pits. Staying stuck in a state of despondency and negative emotions is not an option. Accepting the reality of the estrangement for now and taking steps to reclaim your life, to find peace and even joy again, will not be easy.

But it is possible. Self-ministry, taking care of you and learning new self-help strategies, is hard work. The journey will be filled with ups and downs, but with God's help you can weather the storm.

Remember to "cast your burden on the Lord, and he will sustain you" (Psalm 55:22 ESV). Boldly ask God to bless you with his peace for the present and with hope for the future.

Prayer: *Dear Heavenly Father, we are weary with the brokenness of our families. We are feeling hurt and angry and are filled with sadness and confusion. You have asked us to cast our burdens on you, and you will sustain us. Thank you for that promise. We boldly ask that you bless us with your guidance and your peace on our hearts. In your name we pray, Amen.*

Uncover and Recover

How long must I have sorrow in my heart all the day?

Psalm 13:2 ESV

"Picture perfect" families! We see them all the time on social media posts, annual Christmas card greetings, and sitting in the pew in front of us at church. We conjure up images in our minds of joyful and contented families gathered around a dinner table for holiday celebrations. We may encounter other grandparents at a park or store joyfully keeping watch over their grandchildren. Sign boards with inscriptions such as "family is everything" and "family is the heart of the home" are reminders of our pain and the loss we are experiencing. In reality, no family is perfect.

We are inclined to believe that family troubles happen only in other families, not ours! We think: *a family in turmoil; it can't be mine.* So when difficulties arise, we are in a state of shock, devastation, and disbelief. Mercifully, David reminds us in the book of Psalms (40:2 ESV) that when times were tough, God drew him up from the pit of destruction, out of the miry bog, and set his feet upon a rock, making his steps secure. God can do the same for us. Because we can't stay stuck in brokenness and devastation, it is important to focus on finding peace for the present and moving forward, all the while maintaining hope for the future.

Uncover Family Hurt

Uncover and Recover, Share and Repair, Explore and Restore are all pairs of words connected to the same concept, the notion that it is important to express negative emotions rather than hide them in our hearts or pretend they don't exist. Family hurt hurts! Our hearts will begin to heal only when we confront and deal with the past.

Cry Out to God

You won't be the first person to complain about troubles in your life. The Bible is filled with accounts of believers who uncovered their hurt and opened their hearts to God. In an appeal to God, Job says, "Your hands fashioned and made me, and now you have destroyed me altogether" (Job 10:8 ESV). David lamented, "Why, Lord, do you stand far off? Why do you hide yourself in times of trouble?" (Psalm 10:1 ESV). Again David pleads, "How long must I have sorrow in my heart all the day?" (Psalm 12:2 ESV). An afflicted man moaned, "My heart is struck down like grass and has withered" (Psalm 102:4 ESV). And, as he hangs on the cross, Jesus cries out, "My God, my God, why have you forsaken me?" (Matthew 27:46 ESV).

We can undoubtedly join in the conversation with questions of our own. "Why, Lord, if you are *for* families, did you allow this to happen? Where are you, God? Why haven't you answered my prayers? Why did you bless me with a beautiful family only to take it away?"

The onset of estrangement certainly brings on emotional upheaval. Our minds feel as if they are spinning out of control. The following is a sampling of the adverse emotions experienced by some estranged grandparents:

"Shock, hurt, betrayal, abandonment, brokenness, fear, powerlessness, anger, damaged, bitter, distrustful, unsure, brain fog, lack of concentration...." —Kaye

"Heartbroken...." —Pat

"Bewildered, hopeless, rejected, abused...." —Carolyn

"Accused, blamed, and belittled by our friends...." —Ann

It's no wonder we find ourselves spiraling into a multitude of unmanageable negative thoughts and feelings, overwhelmed by it all.

Identifying Emotions

It's important to pinpoint and put a name on all that we are feeling. How can we begin to accomplish that task when our minds are racing and ruminating with all kinds of negative emotions? Fortunately, our brains are quite complex. It has been established in the past that the right side of our brain is dominant for processing emotions, and the left hemisphere is dominant for processing language. Research [1] has indicated that, in fact, both sides of the brain play a role in processing emotions. The right side of the brain helps us determine "how" an emotion feels, and the left side of the brain provides focus as to the "what." Therefore, both sides of the brain can be engaged to slow our racing minds and help us label our emotions with words. Identifying our feelings is an important first step in processing and coping more effectively.

The collage below is composed of words alienated grandparents have used to label their feelings. Reflect on the words and put a name to some of the emotions you are experiencing.

DISRESPECTED   Humiliated

FEAR   **GRIEF**

Manipulated   Loss of Identity

Invisible   CONFUSION   Frustration

HEARTBROKEN

Powerless   Anger   Shock   DESPAIR

REJECTION   Sadness   DISAPPOINTMENT

Disbelief   **UNFAIRNESS**   ABUSED

Bewilderment   HOPELESSNESS

Helplessness   **HURT**

Managing Emotions

It is not uncommon for estranged grandparents to fear sharing their broken family situation and their hurt with others, as doing so may lead to scrutiny and conviction. Many are ashamed and prefer not to relate the current heartbreaking state of their family to anyone. A great number of grandparents want to withdraw and keep their feelings to themselves.

Interestingly, I observed this behavior of isolation in a lone Canada goose as it hung out by the pond near my home. Day after day, when other geese would flock to the pond, it would never join them. I couldn't help but feel sorry for the creature as it distanced itself from the others. Curiosity got the best of me, and I searched for an answer. I discovered that upon the death of a mate, the surviving goose enters a state of grief and will seclude itself from the flock to grieve alone. Similar to the Canada goose, humans may be inclined to remain disconnected with others who could ultimately offer support.

According to research, withdrawing and suppressing our thoughts and feelings can be harmful. In one study [2], participants who chose to bury their feelings often exhibited stronger stress responses. Hilary Jacobs Hendel, author of *It's Not Always Depression*, states in an article for TIME magazine that "emotional stress, like that from blocked emotions, has not only been linked to mental ills, but also to physical problems like heart disease, intestinal problems, headaches, insomnia, and autoimmune disorders [3]." Overcoming negative emotions is indeed a challenge, but a necessary undertaking.

So, how does one go about managing pain and hurt? As mentioned, one way to express negative emotions is through journaling. Based on an article published by the University of Rochester Medical Center [4], taking time to ponder thoughts and feelings, finding the words to identify them, and writing those words on paper can help us understand them more clearly. The journaling process gives voice to our pain, prioritizes our concerns, and lays the groundwork for developing a plan to manage our hurt. The following example is a reflection from my journal:

Estrangement from my family has been the saddest time of my life. The rejection by my son and daughter-in-law, as well as the alienation from my grandchildren, is agonizing. I have lost my identity as a grandmother, a role that every mother looks forward to and cherishes. The sadness is overwhelming, and the anger just keeps resurfacing. I feel powerless, manipulated, and at a loss. I have worked so hard all these years to nurture a beautiful family, and now my whole world has been upended. I wonder if my life will end on this very sad note.

Initially, the journaling process was something in which I did not want to engage. I deemed the exercise to be pointless and futile. Eventually, I gave way to the blank lines and began writing. I have to say I was mildly surprised to sense a bit of calmness after getting my thoughts down on paper. I was able to identify what was upsetting me, and the whirlwind of emotions in my mind lessened somewhat in intensity.

Think about the emotions you are experiencing, and use a journal to record your feelings. When you are ready, consider setting up a time to meet with a friend, neighbor, or relative to share your pain and begin your journey of healing.

Recover from Family Hurt

The onset of alienation certainly brings untold hurt and heartache. We wonder how and why this situation is even happening in our family. We may find that each day our circumstances are controlling us, and we are only going through the motions of daily life. Our bewildered minds are constantly focused on the sadness, anger, and unfairness of it all. Life is a blur.

It was during my long journey of estrangement that I took time to read a multitude of books in search of answers to the many questions alienation raised. It was important for me to understand why my son and daughter-in-law abruptly abandoned me. Discovering a sure-fire solution for repairing my family became my mission. I also sought advice and counsel from friends and professionals. Efforts to reach out to my alienator in various ways to initiate reconciliation were to no avail. My continued status of abandoned mother and grandmother was very, very disappointing! Eventually, I came to the conclusion that I had to move forward. Remaining in a miserable state every day was not an option. I needed to accept my estrangement situation, for now, and find new purpose for my life. One day on your journey of estrangement, you may also come to the realization that you need to take your life back. It is an understatement to say that process is easier said than done. How does a person know where to begin? How does one change course in life and take a different path than the one so very much anticipated? Purposeful planning plays a crucial role.

Purposeful Plans

Planning, specifically lesson planning, has been a part of my life for many, many years. As a former teacher I have had the opportunity to write thousands of daily lesson plans for my students. Planning necessitates the consideration of all the main components: objectives, materials, procedures, and assessments. Writing lesson plans was not the most enjoyable part of teaching, but the school day was much more positive and productive with a detailed guide in hand. The plans provided structure and purpose for my days in the classroom.

Setting goals and making plans are also important on our road to recovery. They provide structure to our lives and give us a sense of purpose. Instead of remaining stuck in a rut and ruminating in thoughts of hopelessness and despair, a plan can keep us from getting side-tracked and meandering into the miry bog of negative emotions. Similar to a road map, a detailed plan provides clear direction for moving forward.

Think of a goal you could set that brings you peace, happiness, or a sense of purpose. Then identify your objective, the materials you might need, the implementation process, and how you are going to hold yourself accountable. Finally, set a deadline for achieving your goal. Below is an example of a personal goal that may provide some inspiration. Use a journal to begin writing a plan of your own.

- **Objective:** Plan a week of purpose-filled days, something for yourself and something you can do for someone else.
- **Procedure:** Make a list of options, such as volunteer, walk, exercise, garden, complete a project, call someone, read, or bake. Come to a decision and write the plans on your calendar.
- **Materials:** paper, pen, calendar
- **Evaluation:** Reflect on my progress in one week.

For I know the plans I have for you, declares the Lord, plans to prosper you and not to harm you, plans to give you a hope and a future.

(Jeremiah 29:11 ESV)

Lean on God

It is through reading the Bible that we can get to know God and connect with him. He speaks to us through Scripture. Psalm 119:105 reminds us that God's word is a lamp to our feet and a light to our path. Let God's word fill your heart, your mind, and your soul.

Sometimes we wonder where God is in the midst of all this hurt. God may feel far away, but he is really close by our side. I personally experienced the nearness of God during one of my teaching days. I do not recall the topic of the difficult-to-understand lesson for religion class, but I will always remember the assistance I received.

In preparation, I had read over the teacher's manual and decided that there was no way my students would ever comprehend the concepts in the lesson. That evening I thought and thought and thought, but my mind was blank. The next day, shortly before class, I reviewed the teacher's manual again and was still at a loss for words. I had no choice but to proceed with the instructional plan as written. When I got to the confusing point in the lesson, the words that came from my mouth were a perfect explanation of the concept! "YES!" I thought.

There is no doubt in my mind that those words were given to me by the Holy Spirit. The sad part of the story is that I realized I hadn't even considered asking God for help. The truth of God's Word found in Isaiah 65:24 (ESV), "before they call I will answer; while they are yet speaking I will hear," certainly rang true for me that day. The same is true today and always. God is near. We just need to remember to fully rely on him instead of fully relying on our own devices.

Take time to talk to God in prayer. He is listening! Ask God to heal your aching heart, troubled mind, and weary soul. We are reminded in the Bible to "not be anxious about anything, but in every situation, by prayer and petition, with thanksgiving, present your requests to God. And the peace of God, which transcends all understanding, will guard your hearts and minds in Christ Jesus" (Philippians 4:6-7 ESV). Perhaps prayer could be included as a daily goal in your planning. Consider using a prayer journal to write requests for yourself and others, your dreams and goals, blessings you have received, and anything that is on your heart. Keep it in a place where you are reminded to use it daily.

Remember You Are Loved

We are children of God, and we are loved! We are not defined by the hurtful words of others, particularly words of rejection from our adult children. It is important to feel that we are valued as a person and as a grandparent. When we love ourselves and recognize the gifts and talents God has given each of us, love can flow from our hearts to others. Take a few minutes to think about what wonderful attributes and strengths God has given you and write them in your journal. Remember, we are "fearfully and wonderfully made" (Psalm 139:14 ESV).

An added benefit to loving yourself and recognizing that you are a child of God is that you can become a source of comfort to others who are hurting. This concept is stated perfectly in the following Bible verse:

Praise be to the God and Father of our Lord Jesus Christ, the Father of compassion and the God of all comfort, who comforts us in all our troubles, so that we can comfort those in any trouble with the comfort we ourselves receive from God."

(2 Corinthians 1:3-4 NIV)

Hang on to Hope

Life is filled with an abundance of good things such as rainbows, roses, sunsets, music, and laughter. In contrast, we may experience the not-so-good things of life when stress, financial worries, illness, and broken family relationships come our way. We are joyful about all the beautiful parts of life, but we can easily become despondent when life goes downhill.

In 2 Corinthians 11, Paul relates the many trials of his life. He was beaten, stoned, shipwrecked at sea, and faced countless dangers from rivers, robbers, the wilderness, and his own people. Paul experienced sleepless nights, hunger, thirst, and cold. In addition to all those things, Paul faced daily pressure in regards to all the churches he had founded. And yet, while in Corinth, Paul wrote, "we know that in all things God works for the good of those who love him, who have been called according to his purpose" (Romans 8:28 NIV). These words set us free from feelings of desperation and hopelessness to ones of optimism and hopefulness.

Paul uses the words "we know," not "we think" or "perhaps," to convey the certainty that we do indeed have knowledge of the truth, and we can place complete confidence in our God. Our God is a great God, one who is almighty and all-powerful. He created the world and all things in it. He raised Jesus from the dead and won victory over sin and death. God is bigger than all our problems, and we can place our trust in him when challenges and heartaches enter our lives.

We are reminded in Romans 12:12 (ESV) to "rejoice in hope, be patient in tribulation, and be constant in prayer." As we hang on to hope, we can be confident that God is on this journey with us.

Prayer: *Dear Heavenly Father, we thank you for the good memories and positive moments we have had with our loved ones. We ask your help in moving forward toward healing and in finding a path toward reconciliation. Sometimes our strong emotions become a stumbling block. Help us respond to situations with grace and mercy. We ask that you bless us with peace for now and with hope for the future. In your name we pray, Amen.*

Forgiveness

———

Be kind and compassionate to one another, forgiving each other, just as in Christ God forgave you.

Ephesians 4:32 NIV

As estranged grandparents, the very thought of forgiveness may seem inconceivable. How can we forgive those who have alienated and rejected us? How can we forgive those who have accused us of being overbearing and unsupportive? How can we forgive those who have not even offered an apology for their hurtful actions? Our broken hearts most certainly do not feel like forgiving. Yet that is exactly what the Bible tells us to do! We are to "be kind and compassionate to one another, forgiving each other, just as in Christ God forgave you" (Ephesians 4:32 NIV).

The Greek word for forgiveness is "aphiemi," and its translation means to "let go." This implies that our offenders are to be pardoned and released of all debt. The thought of canceling our alienator's debt looms in our minds as an impossibility. When my daughter-in-law made false accusations against me, the first thing that came to mind was definitely not forgiveness. It was revenge! I wanted to hold her accountable for her hurtful words.

Parable of the Unforgiving Servant

God, in his mercy, has forgiven each of us all our sins. Through Jesus' death on the cross, God does not count our sins against us. He wants us to forgive others, just as he has forgiven us. Consider the parable of the unforgiving servant as told by Jesus.

Therefore the kingdom of heaven may be compared to a king who wished to settle accounts with his servants. When he began to settle, one was brought to him who owed him ten thousand talents. And since he could not pay, his master ordered him to be sold, with his wife and children and all that he had, and payment to be made. So the servant fell on his knees, imploring him, "Have patience with me, and I will pay you everything." And out of pity for him, the master of that servant released him and forgave him the debt. But when that same servant went out, he found one of his fellow servants who owed him a hundred denarii, and seizing him, he began to choke him, saying, "Pay what you owe." So his fellow servant fell down and pleaded with him, "Have patience with me, and I will pay you." He refused and went and put him in prison until he should pay the debt. When his fellow servants saw what had taken place, they were greatly distressed, and they went and reported to their master all that had taken place. Then his master summoned him and said to him, "You wicked servant! I forgave you all that debt because you pleaded with me. And should not you have had mercy on your fellow servant, as I had mercy on you?" And in anger his master delivered him to the jailers, until he should pay all his debt. So also my heavenly Father will do to every one of you, if you do not forgive your brother from your heart. (Matthew 18:23-35 ESV)

Most of us would readily agree that the servant in the parable, who himself had been forgiven, should not have imprisoned his debtor. Likewise, we, who also have been forgiven by God, should not seek revenge, but forgive. God extended his grace, and we are commanded to do the same. When we ponder all that God has forgiven us, we are grateful. However, when we ponder all the hurt we have endured at the hands of our alienators, it's really tough to become the one who forgives.

Even so, Paul the Apostle reminds us that "God demonstrates his own love for us in this: while we were still sinners, Christ died for us" (Romans 5:8 NIV). That's what forgiveness is all about—forgiving sinners! Our imperfections and weaknesses did not stop God from accepting us. However, as the servant in the parable, it is distinctly possible that we would also find it very difficult to forgive an imperfect family member who hurt us deeply.

Forgiveness is Hard Work

Forgiving others is one of those topics in the Bible we sometimes just want to skip over. We don't want to read in Colossians 3 that we must put on compassionate hearts and kindness and then forgive. We reason that we are the ones who have been wronged! Our alienators are the ones who should apologize. We want to show them how much pain and heartache they have caused us! We feel they don't deserve to be forgiven. The unfairness of it all is first and foremost on our minds!

However, forgiveness does not mean that we must deny the reality of our offender's hurtful actions. We most definitely need to acknowledge the wrongs against us and the pain inflicted. Martin Luther King Jr. once stated, "Forgiveness does not mean ignoring what has been done or putting a false label on an evil act. It means, rather, that the evil act no longer remains as a barrier to the relationship. Forgiveness is a catalyst creating the atmosphere necessary for a fresh start and a new beginning."

We must recognize that "push and shove" and "blow for blow" scenarios lead nowhere and often make matters worse. The words of Proverbs 12:18(ESV) remind us that "rash words are like sword thrusts, but the tongue of the wise brings healing." In other words, responses of anger allow hate to remain in our hearts and can cause more damage. Eventually, one party needs to be the buffer and put an end to the negative actions and reactions in order to diffuse the situation and lay a foundation for healing.

Interestingly, the act of forgiveness requires only one person—you! Forgiveness is not dependent on receiving apologies from our alienators. Forgiveness is the cancellation of a debt. Unwillingness to forgive causes us to hold on closely to anger, bitterness, and resentment. The Bible reminds us to get rid of all bitterness, rage and anger, brawling and slander, along with every form of malice (Ephesians 4:31 NIV). Otherwise, our hostile hearts will make reconciliation even more challenging and perhaps impossible. In addition, hostile hearts hold us hostage to our alienators which enables them to control our lives and rob us of joy and peace. T.D. Jakes, American pastor and motivational speaker, offers some inspirational thoughts on the freeing power of forgiveness: "Forgiveness liberates the victim. It's a gift you give yourself [1]." Forgiveness softens our hearts and opens the door to reconciliation.

Forgiveness is a Process

Forgiveness is indeed a process! It's hard work that needs to be accomplished in small steps. Consider these words of wisdom from Maya Angelou regarding the concept of embarking on a long, difficult path. "Every great journey starts with a single step." It's important to take some time and give thought to the first step we might take.

Asking God to place the desire to forgive in our hearts is a necessary starting point. Waiting for "time to heal all wounds," and thus lessen the hurt, is not an effective strategy. Waiting for an apology to green light our forgiveness journey is not an option. We will be waiting a long time. We can't control our alienators, but we can control our responses. If our hearts are hardened, we can seek help by going to God in prayer and asking him to change our hearts and give us the strength to forgive. God is able to do that, and he reminds us of that when he says, "I will give you a new heart and put a new spirit in you; I will remove from you your heart of stone and give you a heart of flesh" (Ezekiel 36:26-27 NIV).

Next, we must ponder the offense we need to forgive, label it in our minds with words, and then take time to write it down. Acknowledging the pain and hurt we have experienced as a result of our alienator's actions is a necessary step. Then, we might consider a physical act, such as ripping the paper to pieces or burning it, to visualize our anguish being removed and the debt being released.

Again, forgiveness does not happen overnight. One must work toward forgiveness. There is no button we can press or switch we can flip. God will work in us through the power of the Holy Spirit. We may find that over time (perhaps even hourly or daily), anger and bitterness resurface. We must work continually toward forgiveness. In Matthew 18, Jesus says that we must forgive our debtors, not seven times, but seventy-seven times! Without question, forgiveness is an undertaking that requires time and patience.

Do not take revenge, my dear friends, but leave room for God's wrath, for it is written: "It is mine to avenge; I will repay says the Lord."

(Romans 12:19 NIV)

Family Hurt

Honestly speaking, family hurt just hurts. We are heartbroken that our family is not whole. Regrettably, we are experiencing the result of sin in this world, and we need to remember that God is with us through our pain and suffering. In fact, difficulties in our lives often bring us closer to God. Trust him, even when we want to take the situation into our own hands, and continue to pray. The words in Luke 18:1 (ESV) encourage us "to always pray and not lose heart."

Prayer: *Dear Heavenly Father, we know you understand the hurt we feel as estranged grandparents and the pain of broken family relationships. We ask that you help us release that pain and forgive those who have hurt us, just as you have forgiven us. Heal our hearts with your grace. Amen.*

Reconciliation

If possible, so far as it depends on you, live peaceably with all.

Romans 12:18 ESV

A ccording to the Oxford English dictionary, the definition of reconciliation is "the action of restoring estranged people or parties to friendship." For estranged grandparents, family restoration is the most desired result and the end of a heartbreaking journey. The very thought of reconciliation gives us a sense of hope, puts a song in our hearts, and is music to our ears.

It Takes Two

Just as it takes two to tango and two to play table tennis, it takes *two* to reconcile. Recall that the act of forgiveness takes only *one*—you! Reconciliation is not possible unless both parties are agreeable to finding a path forward in the relationship. Early on in my estrangement, communication was a one-way road. Incoming text messages identifying my negative character traits, along with "evidence" to support the claims, filled my days and weeks. These false accusations abruptly interrupted my life while dining out, having coffee with friends after church, waking up in the morning, and at various times throughout the day. The texts usually concluded with a request to keep my distance, as they (my son and daughter-in-law) were still hurting and not ready to talk. In my situation, the prospect of reconciliation wasn't even remotely on the table. The following statements from other grandparents provide confirmation that reconciliation is not always possible and must involve earnest conversation between two stakeholders:

"I have not been given the opportunity to reconcile." —Pat

"I tried to reach out at Christmas, but I was told lies and to stay away." –Ann

"I have no open communication. I do not feel I can be honest. Fear of loss of more contact with my son stops me. If you can hold back what you have to say until you figure out the best way, I would." –Kaye

Indeed, there are times along the journey of estrangement where reconciliation is not attainable. In those situations we need to turn to God and ask him to help free our hearts from all the anger. Then, with gentler hearts, we will be better prepared to engage in productive dialogue when the opportunity for reconciliation presents itself.

A Biblical Example of Restored Relations

In a conversation with Peter, after Jesus had risen from the dead, Jesus gave us a picture of what the restoration of a broken relationship might look like. Recall that on the day Jesus was crucified, the disciples were disappointed because their hopes in Jesus had vanished, and they were fearful of what might happen to them if they were identified as friends of his. Three times Peter denied knowing Jesus, just as Jesus had predicted. After his resurrection, Jesus approached Peter and asked Peter if he still loved him. Even though Peter had totally abandoned Jesus, the question gave Peter the opportunity to respond that he did indeed love Jesus. Jesus restored his relationship with Peter and demonstrated his belief in him by giving Peter the responsibility to feed his sheep (John 21:15-17). In this account, Jesus reached out to Peter to mend their relationship, and Peter accepted. This is a beautiful example of reconciliation, as the two parties agreed to restore their broken relationship.

Perspectives on Reaching Out

Perhaps by developing an understanding of the thoughts and feelings of our estranged children, we can uncover some of the negative emotions they may be experiencing. We may begin to harbor less resentment and animosity. We are not looking for a reason to excuse their rejection and the resulting heartache; we are only searching for understanding and guidance on the most effective and best ways to communicate with them.

After a couple years of estrangement, I began to realize that my daughter-in-law processed life through her emotions. If she felt something intensely, then it was reality. It brought me back to my teaching days as I recalled the state of mind of students who were under emotional stress due to challenging family situations at home, low self-esteem, or whatever the case may have been. Their right brains, the emotional side, were operating relentlessly, and it was almost impossible for them to focus on the academics. They were reacting to their current circumstances which limited their ability to reason. Those recollections caused me to feel compassion for my daughter-in-law, who was hurting and reacting to life in general. I thought about how difficult it must be for her to go through life that way.

Consider the account of Jesus and Peter. Peter denied knowing Jesus three times! Why? Peter did not want to acknowledge his relationship with Jesus for fear of his own life. Fear controlled Peter's behavior. What might be some factors that control our alienators' behaviors? As stated in chapter one, an influential adversary, such as a son-in-law or daughter-in-law, can be a factor. Mental health concerns such as anxiety, depression, addiction, or alcoholism may play a role. We may not understand the reasons for estrangement from the perspective of our adult children, but we need to realize we cannot change their perspective. We need to come to the understanding that hurt people hurt people. Once again, T.D. Jakes [1, p. 114] offers some insight as to why our alienators have rejected us. "Most people who hurt us weren't really thinking about our needs at all. Most people aren't oriented to consider how their actions affect your well-being. Most people are so focused on their crises and needs that they seem oblivious to what their actions have done to you; their intentions aren't as much against you as they are for them."

Additional Thoughts on Connecting

Many estranged grandparents are in a state of uncertainty when it comes to contacting their adult children. We ponder and perhaps even agonize over the various possibilities facing us. We may ask ourselves some of the following questions: Is this a good time to reach out? Shall I leave things alone for now, or should I contact my adult child? Will my child think I don't love them or care about them if I am silent? Do I think I can handle being rejected again if I do make contact? Is it worth the risk? Am I just enabling my adult child to hurt me again? What is the right approach?

I spent many days pondering the above questions. I had been given instructions by my son and daughter-in-law to keep my distance. They texted me to say they would reach out when *they* were ready. However, as time went on I became concerned about my grandchildren. I had spent a lot of time with them, and I knew the abrupt separation was not a good thing for them. I suggested we meet at a park, a neutral location, for lunch and some play time. The response was no! There I was, rejected again! After several more attempts to connect with my family, I decided the rejection was more painful than remaining silent.

Time passed, and one day I received an email stating that my son and daughter-in-law felt I did not care about them since I had not contacted them for a very long time! They communicated to me that the silent treatment was painful and uncomfortable. Furthermore, they did not feel important! Sometimes we are caught up in no-win situations.

In another scenario, one daughter, who had alienated her mother for several years before eventually reconciling, shared some advice for estranged grandparents—stay in touch. The daughter appreciated the times her mother had reached out with loving messages even though she did not respond.

With regard to connecting with loved ones, circumstances are different for each family, and there is not a universal plan of action for all. If you do decide to contact your adult child, the following section offers some strategies.

A Communication Compass from God

How do we go about reaching out? Grandparent alienation brings with it a flurry of emotions, feelings of anger, and disbelief. The first reactions to our painful circumstances may be ones of defensiveness and feeling the need to explain things from our perspective. We may experience the impulse to seek revenge and express to our alienators the wrongfulness and unfairness of their actions.

After taking a deep breath, as well as some time to reflect, we find ourselves in a state of mental confusion as we consider the best way to respond to this heartbreaking family situation. The Bible offers some thoughts on the matter.

- **Be Quick to Hear and Slow to Speak:** "Know this, my beloved brothers: let every person be quick to hear, slow to speak, slow to anger" (James 1:19 ESV). These words of wisdom suggest that stepping back and pondering a response before communicating is wise. Responding to words of criticism and dismissiveness with anger may further exacerbate our circumstances.

- **Listen:** "Make your ear attentive to wisdom and incline your heart to understand" (Proverbs 2:2 ESV). This is how God wants us to hear his word and how God wants us to listen to others.
- **Speak Gently:** "A hot-tempered person stirs up conflict, but the one who is patient calms a quarrel" (Proverbs 15:18 NIV).
- **Respond with Love:** "But I say to you who hear, love your enemies, do good to those who hate you, bless those who curse you, pray for those who abuse you" (Luke 6:27-28 ESV). Seeking the good in others, understanding that hurt people hurt people, and responding with love all help diffuse the cycle of abusive communication.
- **Forgive:** "Bear with one another and, if one has a complaint against another, forgive each other; as the Lord has forgiven you, so you also must forgive" (Colossians 3:13 ESV).

Experts agree that anger, bitterness, and defensiveness are not effective tools for rebuilding a relationship. The following words of advice from the Bible support that statement: "Don't have anything to do with foolish and stupid arguments, because you know they produce quarrels. And the Lord's servant must not be quarrelsome, but must be kind to everyone, able to teach, not resentful" (2 Timothy 2: 23-24 NIV). Even though it is not an easy task, and it may take time for us to be in a better place, we have the opportunity to demonstrate, or teach, God's love in the midst of situations of conflict.

As mentioned previously, during the first couple years of my estrangement, I received multiple text messages from my daughter-in-law. Each one related a story of how I had hurt her personally, and each one came with an adjective that denigrated me as a person and as a grandmother. I decided to create a word document detailing all the allegations followed by all my rebuttals. That process helped me organize my thoughts and prepare me for a future meeting with my daughter-in-law. I needed to let her know that words such as overbearing, unsupportive, manipulative, and disrespectful did not describe me. I longed to defend myself and to offer explanations such as "that was not my intent, my actions have been misperceived, you have rewritten history, and that's just not true." After all the time and efforts put forth in creating my talking points, I never did meet with my daughter-in-law. I had come to the conclusion that sharing my defensive words would be a useless endeavor and not lead to reconciliation. However, I will say that the painstaking act of journaling my thoughts helped me process my pain and my feelings of anger.

In fact, reaching out when our hearts remain hostile may give our alienators reason to continue the estrangement. Thus, we really can't connect until our hearts are in a better place and free from animosity. The Bible tells us to love our enemies and pray for those who mistreat us (Luke 6: 27-28 NIV). Human nature makes it very difficult for us to implement the instructions outlined in those Bible verses. We need help. God hears our prayers, and we can ask him to guide our hearts and minds as we discern the best path forward in communicating with our loved ones.

Thoughts on Amends Letters

Although reaching out in person is the best option, we may wonder if it is advisable to share our thoughts, our apologies, and our wishes for reconciliation in the form of a written letter. Experts have various opinions on the effectiveness and soundness of writing amends letters. Author and certified life coach, Sheri McGregor [2, p. 262] contends that the act of apologizing may indeed open doors to communication and understanding *if* there is a caring relationship. However, McGregor believes that apologizing may not be productive, or even make matters worse, if the relationship is one-sided. Conversely, author and psychologist, Dr. Joshua Coleman [3, p. 209], believes that letters of amends demonstrate that one cares.

Certainly if we have done something wrong or hurtful, we must choose the honorable path and apologize. We should make the first move, acknowledge our part in the situation, express regret, commit to changing our ways, and ask for forgiveness.

However, if they initiated the estrangement, we may be thinking it would be more fitting for our adult children to reach out to us to initiate an apology. In all likelihood, that will not happen. Even though it seems unfair, we will need to practice patience, employ understanding, and begin working toward reconciliation. Recall the biblical account of Peter denying Jesus and jeopardizing their relationship. Even though Peter was the one who had wronged Jesus, Jesus was the one who approached Peter to renew the relationship. We will need to pray and ask God for wisdom and strength to take those first steps toward mending our broken relationship.

What about the scenario in which grandparents are accused of not accepting responsibility for hurting their adult child's feelings? What if grandparents feel they have been falsely accused? Author and leading authority on family relationships Gregory Jantz [4, p. 74], believes one should take responsibility only for their part in the broken relationship and not accept false guilt from others. The text found in Proverbs 19:19 (ESV) reinforces that concept with these words: "a man of great wrath will pay the penalty, for if you deliver him, you will only have to do it again." In other words, if we accept blame for something we did not do, we are most likely enabling the abuse and false accusations to continue. Sometimes, no matter how hard and how long one tries to communicate, a person will persist in deflecting, blaming, and avoiding, rather than taking ownership of the conflict. The inability to recognize or own the problem prevents any change, growth, or resolution from occurring. Consequently, reconciliation may have to be put on hold for the time being.

My own experience with writing an amends letter to my daughter-in-law was not productive. I wrote the apology letter at the request of my son because he thought it would help initiate first steps towards reconciliation. In my correspondence, I accepted blame for all the allegations against me and asked for my daughter-in-law's forgiveness so that we could move forward. A few friends and family members reviewed the letter and provided feedback. After several revisions, I mailed the letter and waited patiently for a response. In the end, I received no acknowledgement of the receipt of my amends letter and no response as to its content.

Unfortunately, there are no easy answers when it comes to the question of the merit of amends letters. The best option is to weigh the advice from the experts presented above and make the best decision possible for your situation.

The Road to Reconciliation

The journey of grandparent alienation and estrangement could very well be a long, bumpy road. One day we hope to reach the desired destination of reconciliation and renewed family bonds.

Psychologist and author Dr. John Townsend [5], in an interview with *Focus on the Family*, laid out an approach to reconciliation that he feels offers the best hope of a positive outcome. He suggests setting up a meeting with your adult child with the promise you will listen, and only listen, to *their* concerns. Tell your adult child that you will take those concerns home with you, write them down, pray about them, and change anything they said that was true. Then, at a second meeting, share how you have changed and want to stay changed. Hopefully, this line of action will begin to open the door toward reconciliation.

The first step is to make contact with your alienator to set up a time to connect. Face-to-face is the most effective. Because in-person contact is not always possible for estranged grandparents, a phone call or video call is the next best option. Text messages, emails, and handwritten letters are alternate choices, but be mindful that text does not communicate as much information as face-to-face contact. Text can be misinterpreted if they don't know your tone and intentions. Begin by setting the foundation for your meeting, and be clear about your intentions. Just as travelers need road maps, estranged grandparents need written plans. Prepare your talking points on paper before communicating with your adult child. Topics might include a statement about your desire to reconnect and about your commitment to listening. Following is an example of how one might lay the groundwork and set up a meeting:

As my son and daughter-in-law, I want you to know that you mean the world to me. Your children, each one so special, are also very precious to me. I understand that as parents, you are number one in your children's lives. I acknowledge there has been a great distance between us the last few years and that is not where I want to be in our relationship. I am praying for a better relationship in the future. I want to give you the opportunity to express your concerns, and I will promise to listen to all you have to say. Can we find a time and place to meet?

If your adult child agrees to meet, allow them to choose a neutral location where they are most comfortable.

Bring a positive attitude and a proper mindset to the get-together. Experts suggest that we leave any grievances we would love to express at home, or any bridge building that has occurred will collapse. Our past hurts need to remain in the past, at least for now. One estranged grandparent shared that her daughter did not accept her amends letter apology for the sole reason that she believed her mother was not even cognizant of what she had done wrong. Our adult children want us to understand their feelings and their perspective of the relationship. They don't want to hear defensiveness from us; they want empathy. Honestly, they are not interested in our perspective. During the meeting, be mindful of your body language. Maintain eye contact and remember that uncrossed arms signal active listening. The words from Proverbs 2:2 (ESV) offer some sound advice: "incline your heart to understanding."

Another thing to leave behind is the word "but." We will not change our adult child's perspective with any statement that begins with that word. "*But* you don't understand, *but* that's not what happened, *but* that's not what I meant" are all non-starters. Perhaps, one day, our adult children will see our side of the story. For now, as inequitable and unfair as it is, we have to walk on eggshells.

During your time together, ask your adult child or alienator to share their thoughts and concerns. Ask questions to further understand their perspectives. For the purpose of clarification, reflect back to them what you understand their concerns to be. Discuss areas of contention and how they might be resolved. Set a time to meet again to share changes you have decided to make, and if possible, to determine next steps toward reconciliation. Thank them for meeting with you and sharing their thoughts.

If at any time during the meeting, the conversation gets a little stormy, ask your adult child to talk a bit more softly. If the conversation remains blustery, explain that you can hear and process things better when the atmosphere is calmer. Suggest that you meet at another time. Just as travelers must discontinue their journey during inclement weather, it is possible that the road to reconciliation may have to be delayed for a time.

Hold on to Hope

Feelings of hopelessness can easily fill our hearts. We wonder why God has not answered our prayers. We wonder how long this season of our life will last, and we wonder why it even happened. It is truly difficult for us to trust God and wait for his perfect timing. Nonetheless, we must remember that our God is powerful and "is able to do immeasurably more than all we ask or imagine, according to his power that is at work within us" (Ephesians 3:20 NIV). Our God is a God of hope.

Prayer: *Dear Heavenly Father, our hearts are heavy over our broken relationships with our children and grandchildren. Guide our hearts and minds as we make decisions on how best to navigate our circumstances. We pray that you would bless us with healing and reconciliation. In your name we pray, Amen.*

Setting Boundaries in Love

———

Each one must give as he has decided in his heart, not reluctantly or under compulsion, for God loves a cheerful giver.

2 Corinthians 9:7 ESV

Published in 1964, *The Giving Tree* [2] by Shel Silverstein, has become one of his best-known books. The story details the life of the Giving Tree, which is none other than an ordinary apple tree. The Giving Tree loved a little boy and allowed him to swing from its branches and eat its apples. The little boy came to love the tree. Time passed and years later the boy returned to the lonely apple tree to ask for some money. Of course, the apple tree had no money, but the tree responded by giving the boy its fruit to sell. Again, time passed and periodically the boy would return to the apple tree and make an appeal for something to fulfill his heart's desire. The apple tree always consented. The tree gave the grown up young man his branches so he could build a house for his wife and children. When the young man became an old man, the Giving Tree offered him his trunk so he could build a boat and sail away. Finally, after a very long time, the older man returned to the lonely apple tree for a place to sit and rest. The Giving Tree eagerly provided all it had left, its stump.

The title of the book, *The Giving Tree,* causes one to focus on the generosity of the apple tree and the virtue of giving of oneself to enrich the happiness of others. We might have great admiration for the tree for being a selfless example of giving while expecting nothing in return. One could characterize that as unconditional love. As we reflect on the character traits of both the Giving Tree and the boy, we may begin to wonder about this relationship. One could most definitely describe the apple tree as loving, caring, generous, and selfless. On the other hand, the boy might be described as greedy, spoiled, unappreciative, and selfish. One might begin to question whether a relationship in which one person gives generously, and the other person takes selfishly, is a healthy one. These thoughts are worth pondering as we explore the concept of setting boundaries in love.

Boundaries, You, and Your Little Corner of the World

During my childhood years, my father, a bricklayer, built a home for our family. Of course the house was made of brick, and it was situated on a corner lot. The property lines were defined by a sidewalk on the south side, a sidewalk on the west side, a tree line and some perennials on the north side, and a mowing line on the east side. My dad affectionately referred to this space as "my little corner of the world."

We all have a "little corner of the world." Think about what you might find within the property lines, or boundaries, of your domain. Surely you would find yourself. But you would also find what defines you, your identity. Your values, beliefs, thoughts, opinions, decisions, attitudes, goals, feelings, heart, money, time, talents, and abilities are all part of you, your property, and are all within your boundaries. All of these belongings can be categorized into three separate groups as depicted below:

- **Mental:** Values, Beliefs, Thoughts, Goals, Decisions, Attitudes, Opinions
- **Emotional:** Feelings, Your Heart
- **Resources:** Money, Time, Talents, Abilities

Boundaries are the foundation of healthy relationships and help define the story of our lives. Think about the tale of the Giving Tree. The tree gave and gave and gave until it was nothing but a stump. The apple tree's attribute of generosity is certainly admirable, but should the apple tree have allowed the boy to shape the journey of its life so profoundly?

Boundaries Unraveled

Personally, I was taken aback by my daughter-in-law's use of the word boundaries in addressing her concerns with me. She boldly stated that I had crossed *her* boundaries, and consequently, she needed to set boundaries for *me* to observe and respect. She felt compelled to establish a new baseline with me, and apparently a new set of expectations would accomplish that purpose. I was presented with a series of rules to follow regarding any future contact with her, my son, and my grandchildren. WHAT? The whole conversation conjured up feelings of anger within me. How dare anyone give rules to another person!

Confusion filled my mind as I had never heard "boundaries" used in this context before. Many grandparents have also expressed feelings of bewilderment when their alienators have used the term boundaries to confront them. Most of us are of the understanding that a boundary is a line that separates two entities. We can relate to the examples of how political boundaries separate countries. Rivers, mountain ranges, and oceans serve as physical boundaries between regions. Boundaries of basketball courts, tennis courts, and volleyball courts separate the playing surfaces from the out-of-bounds areas. However, the use of phrases such as "you crossed my boundaries" and "now here are your boundaries" clearly indicates that the term has indeed taken on new meaning.

A little research shed some light on this present-day usage of the term. The Washington Post [3] recently published an article entitled "Everyone is setting boundaries. Do they even know what it means?" Evidently the term became popular in the 1990's, spurred by self-help books that became best sellers. The implementation of personal boundaries was intended to refer to the limits we set for ourselves, not rules we impose on others to control their behavior. I came to realize that my daughter-in-law was erroneous in using boundaries synonymously with the word rules. Instead, boundaries are to be defined as personal relational guidelines we set for *ourselves*.

Boundary Considerations

Call to mind again the story of *The Giving Tree* and ponder the following questions. Do you think the apple tree should have set some boundaries for the boy? Why do you think the tree did not set any boundaries? How might the apple tree's life have been different if it had set some boundaries in love for the boy? How might the boy's life have been different if the apple tree had set some boundaries for him?

As estranged grandparents, we may be suffering from ongoing verbal abuse, attacks on our character, or unending requests for financial assistance. How might our lives be different if we seek to establish boundaries for ourselves? Why might we be reluctant to set some boundaries? At what point do we need to begin thinking about setting some parameters for our estranged family members? These questions are worthy of our consideration.

Like the Giving Tree, we grandparents have a spirit of giving. Oftentimes we give and keep on giving because we feel we have to or because we fear losing contact with our children and grandchildren. The words of 2 Corinthians 9:7 (ESV) reinforce the concept that giving should be voluntary and not done unwillingly. "Each one must give as he has decided in his heart, not reluctantly or under compulsion, for God loves a cheerful giver." In other words, we should not give because we feel obligated.

We often feel we should take on the hurts imposed on us and just handle them. But protecting ourselves from the consequences of the hurtful and abusive behavior of others is not selfishness. It is a means of taking care of ourselves and keeping our hearts strong so that we can express love and empathy for others. The words of wisdom found in Proverbs 4:23 (NIV) substantiate that thought: "Above all else, guard your heart, for everything you do flows from it."

On a personal note, the continual onslaught of disrespectful and disparaging text messages I received shattered the very essence of my person. My identity as a loving, caring grandmother had been erased. It was by far the most heartbreaking experience of my life. I felt hurt and misunderstood. I wanted to defend myself, but I was sure that would be to no avail. I thought long and hard about how to respond. I chose silence. Why? I thought I should be the grown up and not retaliate with an "eye for an eye" or a "tooth for a tooth" response. I am also one who attempts to avoid conflict. Above all else, I didn't want to lose the only connection to my grandchildren. "This can't go on forever," "I can forgive," and "I can handle it" were thoughts I used to rationalize away the sadness and hurt. In retrospect, it's possible that I was only enabling the abuse to continue. Proverbs 19:19 (ESV) reminds us that "a man of great wrath will pay the penalty, or if you deliver him, you will only have to do it again." I believe I was prolonging my pain and preventing my alienator from being directed on a new route to seek out and confront the real causes of her anger and unhappiness. Looking back, it would have been wise for me to set some boundaries for myself.

In due time, we may come to the realization that we cannot control others, specifically our alienators, and we should not allow others to control us. Establishing personal limits with others creates a level of understanding and respect. Setting boundaries encourages wholesome relationships by forming healthy mindsets and improving one's mental and emotional well-being. The bottom line is that setting boundaries promotes positive interactions and is a measure to be considered.

A Road Map for Setting Boundaries

Determining boundaries to set requires thoughtfulness and planning. The following road map may be helpful:

- *Acknowledge the Need—First of all, take time to contemplate and evaluate your journey of grandparent alienation. If you come to the realization that you are being controlled, manipulated, or abused, setting a boundary or two with love may provide you a bit of respite along the way. Setting boundaries allows you to remove negative emotions from your property.*
- *Recognize That Setting Boundaries is Difficult—If you are a giving, kind-hearted soul, setting boundaries may be just plain uncomfortable. Pleasing others is something that may be very important to you and something that has become a priority in your relationships, even if it occurs at the expense of your own needs. Changing course is truly difficult.*
- *Identify a Key Boundary—Once you have determined that setting a boundary is necessary, give thought to the boundary you need to put in place. Consider the main goal you hope to accomplish. Keep it simple. Write it down.*
- *Communicate Using "I" Statements—When communicating boundaries, the use of "I" statements gives us the opportunity to talk about our feelings rather than assign blame to our alienators. For example, "I feel heartbroken and hurt when I*

receive your text messages because they devalue my identity as a loving grandma. Therefore, I cannot accept your text messages at this time." This approach helps soften the message that needs to be conveyed and could potentially open the door for further conversation.

- *Remember the Distinction between Boundaries and Rules—A boundary is a statement used to protect you and your own decisions. A rule is a restriction placed on another person. "I feel heartbroken and hurt when I receive your text messages because they devalue my identity as a loving grandmother; therefore, I cannot accept your text messages at this time" is an example of a boundary. "Don't send me any more hurtful text messages" is an example of a rule.*
- *Be Kind and Direct—It is very possible that we will feel some level of anger in the process of communicating a boundary to a loved one. But we absolutely need to keep our composure. Remain calm and factual. Any display of indignation or resentment will carry the message that our alienators are on our property, within our boundaries, and still in control.*
- *Practice—Practice with a friend or in front of a mirror.*
- *Set Consequences—If the boundaries you communicate are broken, be prepared to implement consequences. Your boundaries need to be respected.*

Return to *The Giving Tree*

The Giving Tree gave and gave and gave, until it was just a stump. It gave up its very existence and the opportunity to be fruitful year after year. The Giving Tree was altogether selfless, while the boy conceivably could be considered altogether selfish, controlling, and manipulative. Might the moral of this story connect with the concept of setting boundaries in love? Was the Giving Tree enabling the boy's selfish behavior? What if the apple tree had suggested that the boy take some of its apple seeds and plant more apple trees? Would the apple tree have fostered a sense of responsibility and independence in the boy? The young man would have been able to produce food for his family, gather apples to sell, and have wood to build his house. As estranged grandparents, it might be worth taking time to consider our individual situations and determine if setting boundaries in love is in the best interests of both parties.

Prayer: Lord, teach us how to love the people in our lives who have hurt us. Give us the strength and courage to set boundaries in love when needed. Guard our hearts so that love can overflow to others. Thank you for sending your Holy Spirit to be with us always. Amen

Family Dynamics

Be joyful in hope, patient in affliction, constant in prayer.

Romans 12:12 ESV

The alienation of just one grandparent affects a multitude of family members. Not only immediate family members, such as the spouse, children, and adult siblings, but extended family members including aunts, uncles, cousins, and in-laws are drawn into this heartbreaking state of affairs. Many experience emotions of anger, sadness, and confusion, very much like the rejected grandparent. Questions arise. Shall I become the middle man and try to help with reconciliation? If I talk to the alienator, am I being disloyal? Shall I invite both parties to our family get-together? A considerable amount of family drama is generated as everyone feels the need to tread carefully.

The Bible is filled with directives on how families should be families. Honor your father and mother (Exodus 20:12), train up a child in the way he should go (Proverbs 22:6), obey your parents (Colossians 3:20), husbands love your wives, and wives respect your husbands (Ephesians 5:25) are all instructions for the making of a "perfect" family. Nevertheless, the Bible is filled with many stories of broken families, the families of Adam and Eve, Lot, Isaac, Jacob, and King David to name a few. A broken family is nothing new. But when it's our family, it's hard to comprehend the reality of the situation and difficult to determine a path forward.

This chapter contains a multitude of statements from siblings and other family members articulating their thoughts on various topics. Their words offer perspectives and insights into the effects of alienation and estrangement on the family unit.

A Myriad of Topics, A Myriad of Thoughts

Emotions

"Initially I was mostly angry, confused, and in disbelief. The estrangement seemed pointless and not worth the emotional energy, especially because it caused so much collateral damage to relationships. It was also embarrassing, so it was not something that I shared with friends or coworkers, unless it was a close friend."

"During the worst times, I felt, primarily, worry and anger. Worry stemmed from almost every family interaction. I worried about the next thing my sibling or my mom was going to say in a phone call or text message. I worried about my brother and his family's well-being, as well as my parents' mental and physical well-being."

"I felt angry because I saw the injustice of the situation, and I felt powerless to change it."

"I felt sad for my loved ones who were affected by the abuse."

"I felt as if I was walking on eggshells, fearful that comments I made might hurt a family member."

"Emotionally, I became more anxious and fearful than usual. I did not realize how much anxiety can affect a person physically. I sometimes woke up with a gut-

wrenching feeling in the pit of my stomach."

Changes in Relationships

"I tended to get snippy with my parents when we discussed it, because many times I just did not want to talk about it. Talking about the situation was not going to change anything and would just make me feel worse."

"I worried about how my actions or inactions would impact all the members of my family. I worried that I was not doing enough and that I was saying and doing the wrong things."

"My relationship with my niece probably suffered a bit, partly because I didn't want to appear to be too close to her because my parents couldn't be. I also worried about getting close and then becoming estranged myself."

"I worried that my nieces and nephews would be deprived of the support that an extended family could offer. I was concerned that they were being lied to about their family, they wouldn't know how much we loved them, and they were missing out on the childhood they deserved."

Thoughts Regarding the Estranged Sibling

"In some ways, I felt like I had lost my brother, especially when he could not communicate with our family freely because of restrictions placed on him by his wife. I felt like I could not talk to the 'the real him' anymore. I grieved our relationship even though I knew he was still there."

"Many times during the estrangement, my brother's actions did not appear logical or true to his character."

"I definitely felt more calloused toward my sibling and his family; our relationship had turned into something different."

New Roles

"I felt responsible for my parents' emotional state and often tried to talk my mom out of her feelings or conclusions about the situation."

"I had never before been put in a position where I felt I had to 'defend' my parents."

"I often found myself advising both my alienator sibling and my parents. I felt a bit like a therapist or a mediator, hearing all sides, and trying to facilitate communication between the two without making the situation any worse."

"I suddenly felt like an only child. With one sibling and his family estranged and the other living in another state, I was the only one left for family gatherings. Being an only child is lonely. I felt like I was very boring to my parents compared to the grandkid time they used to have before the alienation."

"I did feel some pressure to be there for my parents, but that pressure came from me and not my parents. I think in some ways the estrangement has brought us closer together."

"I worried about my parents and the hurt they felt. I tried to listen to them, console them, and reassure them that I would always be loyal."

"I felt I had to be the catalyst for some family get-togethers to happen."

Thoughts on How Siblings Felt Parents Have Responded

"After going through years of this family estrangement, there seemed to be no easy solutions. When every action or inaction could set off emotions and tension again, everyone felt stuck and unable to move forward. We all handled the situation as best we could."

"There was always some optimism from my parents. It came in waves for sure, but the optimism shone through. My mother went digging for answers and really tried to find the 'why' for all of this. She was determined to not accept this as a new reality."

The words from family members caught up in the tangled web of family estrangement paint a difficult journey for them, too. They are feeling anger, disbelief, confusion, fear, and embarrassment. Anxiety sets in, and they feel as if they are walking on eggshells. Some feel guilty about the relationships they are still entitled to, while their parents remain abandoned. Some are estranged themselves. Family members worry that the children involved won't know how much they are loved by their extended family and are fearful of the lies they may be hearing. The alienator, their loved one, seems unrecognizable and not the warmhearted, caring sibling they thought they knew. Family members also feel caught in the middle as they assume new roles as advisors and mediators. Estrangement does indeed have far-reaching effects into the family unit.

Communication

Estrangement sets the stage for the likelihood of poor communication, as emotions tend to be strong on both sides. A survey [1] was conducted regarding the extent of communication that actually transpired between any one person and the estranged member of the family. Results indicate that most people tend to avoid the topic of the alienation itself and maintain some measure of physical distance. Many feel uneasy and fear the negative reactions that may occur. However, if one allows avoidance and apprehension to prevail, communication is most certainly hindered and that could eventually initiate a breakdown in understanding and relationships. According to an article in *Scientific American Mind* [2], suppressing thoughts and feelings can be harmful. In one study, participants who chose to bury their feelings often exhibited stronger stress responses.

Clearly, family estrangement is a delicate matter when it comes to communication. Personally, at the onset of my estrangement, I chose to hide the fact that my family was broken. I was ashamed and embarrassed. However, as time passed, sharing my hurts with other family members became a source of healing.

Sharing Burdens

From my perspective as an estranged grandparent, I am grateful for family members who chose to listen and validate my feelings of hurt, which were, in fact, very real. Some tried to talk me out of my feelings, and I resented their lack of empathy. However, I believe they had my best interests at heart and just wanted everything to be all right. On the other hand, I also witnessed the pain and agony on the faces of some confidants and wished I had not burdened them with my family's depressing story.

Sharing burdens with other family members can place estranged grandparents in a bit of a quandary. Unloading all the heartaches and burdens of estrangement on adult children can lead to emotional exhaustion. Take note of these thoughts from siblings of alienators.

"I sometimes became overwhelmed, feeling like I needed to be a therapist for everyone around me. I became an emotional dumping ground."

"There was some friction between my mom and me regarding how much to talk about the situation. We talked about it nearly every time I visited, which caused emotions to surface that I had successfully put aside earlier in the week. I often had a hard time calming myself down afterwards. I would not sleep well and would go into my Monday work week feeling depressed."

"It was frustrating when our family situation seemed to be the only topic of conversation. It was the 'elephant in the room,' and it became exasperating to continually have this on my mind."

Adult children may feel overwhelmed by the pain and wish to distance themselves from their parents. Conversely, suppressing feelings and never talking about the situation is not a healthy alternative either. Striking a balance is the ultimate goal.

Generally speaking, communication among parents, adult children, and other family members should be truthful and straightforward. It's all right to acknowledge the state of brokenness, as well as to express hope for reconciliation and restored family relations. Expressions of sadness, disbelief, and anger, as well as the unfairness of the estrangement situation, are encouraged. But family members should also feel free to take a break from all the negative conversation and resulting apprehensiveness. Compassion and sensitivity, as well as honesty, are important in any dialogue. Without question, it's a difficult path to navigate.

Caught in the Middle

The very nature of family estrangement causes adult children and other family members to be caught in the middle. They are often conflicted, experiencing feelings of disloyalty to the alienated family member if they maintain a relationship with the alienator. Following are some statements from family members who have found themselves in this awkward and problematic situation:

"I constantly felt guilty for maintaining my relationship with my brother's family while my parents were estranged. This caused me so much guilt that I often did not want to talk with my parents about time I had spent with their grandchildren, especially about the grandchild they barely knew."

"I often felt exhausted trying to manage the communication channels between all parties—siblings, kids, and parents."

"We attended a family wedding. It was an awkward situation, but I supported my alienated sister by not speaking at all to her son and family who have treated her so unfairly."

In regards to estranged grandparents themselves, because they have experienced so much hurt, it is understandable that they may tend to seek allegiance from other family members. However, it really is best if alienated parents and grandparents focus on the family they do have in their lives and not expect anyone to choose sides.

Family Boundaries

As discussed in the previous chapter, protection from the consequences of the hurtful and abusive behaviors of others is not selfishness. It is a means of taking care of oneself.

Recall that personal boundaries refer to the limits we set for ourselves, not rules we impose on others to control their behavior. Setting boundaries results in a healthy mindset, and is as needed for us as it is helpful for our alienators. It is no wonder that siblings and other family members are confused when influential adversaries become gatekeepers, denying access to their loved ones, and seem to have so much control. They find it difficult to understand why the gatekeeper's spouse or relative does not take the initiative to set some boundaries to curb the ongoing abusive behaviors. Following are some thoughts from two siblings addressing the topic of inaction.

"I was angry at my brother at times for supporting his wife's illogical and hurtful actions."

"Does my sibling not understand the gravity of alienation? How could he feign that everything is okay while his spouse cuts him and his children off from his family?"

From personal experience and from the stories of others, including a former alienator, the acquiescence to the manipulator might have been done out of necessity. Supporting the gatekeeper kept the atmosphere at home a bit less contentious and helped protect the children as much as possible. Needless to say, family estrangement effectuates a complex state of affairs.

Forgiveness and Mending Fences

It is extremely difficult for adult children and family members to forgive, sit back, and do nothing when they perceive firsthand the hurt and heartache of their broken family and extended family. Considering themselves a neutral party, they may feel they have a responsibility to offer some assistance in repairing the relationship. Consider the following thoughts from extended family members:

"I felt guilty that I had been unable to bring the family back together."

"Eventually I accepted the situation and was less angry because I realized that there was not much I could control. Trusting other people in my family to take care of themselves was a big step in reducing my fear and anger about the estrangement."

Well-meaning family members can actually make matters worse by giving the alienators a piece of their mind or trying to resolve the conflict. The chances of reconnecting with estranged family members will become more of a possibility if compassion and empathy are communicated, rather than judgment. Contemplate the following piece of advice from one sibling:

"Maintain communication. Be neutral and positive. Avoid being reactive even if the alienator in your family responds emotionally or unkindly to you."

God's Word reminds us to "let all bitterness and wrath and anger and clamor and slander be put away from you, along with all malice. Be kind to one another, tenderhearted, forgiving one another, as God in Christ forgave you" (Ephesians 4:31-32 ESV).

Family Plans Going Forward

Undoubtedly, reconciliation is the most desirable outcome possible. Remember that the restoration of a relationship takes two. Both parties must be agreeable to finding a path forward in a relationship, otherwise reconciliation is out of the question. The path to reconciliation is not an effortless endeavor. Kathleen Smith, author of *Understanding the Heartbreak of Family Estrangement*, writes the following: "Reconciliation after estrangement is not an easy thing. In his research, Pillemer, a psychology professor at Cornell, found that family members were most likely to reconcile when people were less fixated on reaching the same understanding of past events and more focused on building a better future together. When people were able to lower their expectations, but also set clear boundaries in the relationship, relationships also tended to improve [3]."

Reconciliation, something for which we have been hoping for and praying for, may very well happen at some point in the future. Until then, the following comments made by family members enduring the heartache of family estrangement offer some advice.

"Value and spend time with the friends and family members that you are speaking to; don't get so bogged down in the consequences of the estrangement that it trumps every other relationship."

"Do something constructive with your day that does not involve the estrangement, such as volunteering or spending time with friends. It makes a positive impact on others and helps you remember that the estranged family member is just one part of your life. Right now you can't change the situation, but there are many areas of your life that you can change. Take action on what you can change rather than agonizing over what you can't. You may find that it improves your mental health and confidence, and it gives you something to do while you wait."-

"Remain positive. Don't be afraid to share your situation; you are not alone. This situation can feel so personal when in reality it's not really about you. It is likely that your actions could not have prevented this. So do your best to continue living your life. Find joy in the many things that are going well for you."

Focus on the family you *do* have in your life. Rather than remaining stuck in the realm of sadness and grief, carry on with your family traditions or be creative and establish some new ones. It doesn't mean that you can never talk through the hurts of family estrangement. However, do find time to celebrate as a family. Take time to plan activities that meet the interests of everyone. Set the dates, enjoy the time together, and cherish the new memories.

Reach Out to Our Repairer, Rebuilder, and Redeemer

The yearning to repair our broken relationship will most likely remain strong and heartfelt. Questions will continue to arise as to how to diffuse the conflict and restore the family to wholeness. After months and years of estrangement, we may feel inadequate and powerless in our abilities to fix our family. We may feel that the task is not one we can handle on our own, and we are inclined to reach out for help. But, where do we go? For a splintered bone we call a reputable doctor, for faulty brakes we seek out a quality mechanic, and for leaky pipes we contact a highly-rated plumber. But who specializes in repairing, rebuilding, and redeeming broken families? God does!

We can call on God for comfort and guidance. We know that he is "near to the brokenhearted and saves the crushed in spirit" (Psalm 34:18 ESV). We can turn to God in prayer and ask him to heal our fractured family. "For nothing will be impossible with God" (Luke 1:37

ESV). We can trust that God is working to restore what is broken in our family according to his timing and in his way.

Be joyful in hope, patient in affliction, constant in prayer.

(Romans 12:12 ESV)

Prayer: *Dear Heavenly Father, the brokenness of our family feels overwhelming and hopeless. We thank you that you have promised to be with us always. We pray that you rebuild our family and bestow upon us a lasting reconciliation. Our hope and trust is in you. In your name we pray, Amen.*

Letting Go and Letting God

———

Trust in the Lord with all your heart, and do not lean on your own understanding. In all your ways acknowledge him, and he will make straight your paths.

Proverbs 3:5-6 ESV

It is human nature to want to be in control of all situations, as we fear the outcomes will not be what we hoped for or anticipated. It's when the clouds roll in, the winds blow fiercely, and the torrential rains pour down that reality sets in, and we are reminded that we do *not* have control over everything. When the storms of life come our way, trusted friends might give us the advice to "let go and let God." Our response, spoken or unspoken, may be something like "yeah, right" or "easier said than done." So how is the saying "let go and let God" to be interpreted? There are two directives given in this common phrase often used to offer counsel, and the answers are found in God's Word.

Let Go

- **Let Go of Control**—"Trust in the Lord with all your heart, and do not lean on your own understanding" (Proverbs 3:5 ESV).
- **Let Go of Worry**—"Do not be anxious about anything" (Philippians 4:6 ESV).
- **Let Go of Doubt**—"But when you ask, you must believe and not doubt, because the one who doubts is like a wave of the sea, blown and tossed about by the wind" (James 1:6 NIV). Pray with the faith and conviction that our God is powerful

and loving.

- **Let Go of Burdens**—"Cast your burden on the Lord, and he will sustain you" (Psalm 55:22 ESV).

Let God

- **Let God Renew Your Mind**—Put your worries aside, and "be transformed by the renewal of your mind" (Romans 12:2 ESV).
- **Let God Give You Strength**—"God is our refuge and strength, a very present help in trouble" (Psalm 46:1 ESV).
- **Let God Do the Impossible**—God is "able to do immeasurably more than all we could possibly ask or imagine, according to his power that is at work within us" (Ephesians 3:20 NIV). Take note of the words "at work within us." "Letting God" does not mean that we just turn everything over to God and sit and wait for him to do the work. You may have heard the expression "God doesn't move parked cars!" Rather, the power of the Holy Spirit is at work alongside us and within us. The Holy Spirit guides us and comforts us through God's Word, through various resources, and through other people in our lives. In the process of letting go of our hurt and pain, the Holy Spirit steers us on our journey.

Giving up Control

I know in my heart that God wants me to cast my burdens and my worries on him, but when there is a problem, I tend to default to fixer mode. I want to take control and find a solution. When my students were struggling with reading, I researched and researched until I uncovered some new strategies to implement. When critters began nibbling and pulling my freshly planted animal-proof perennials out of the ground, I sprang into action. Plant protectors, stakes with bird netting, cayenne pepper, and organic sprays were all part of the relatively unsuccessful attempts to save my plants. And, of course, when my children were growing up, I fixed the physical hurts with bandages and the emotional hurts with hugs. When I became an alienated grandparent, I wanted to do everything I could to fix the problem and make it go away. I thought, "Certainly God doesn't want my family to be shattered in pieces." However, after much time had passed, I recognized that my attempts to repair my broken family were futile, and I finally had to "let go" and "let God."

How do we go about "letting God" when we have such a strong desire to lean on our own understanding and fix our problems? If an instruction manual for "Letting God" actually existed, step one would clearly state—pray! The first action we need to take is to talk to God and share our troubling family situations. We need to ask him for guidance, strength, peace, and healing. He is listening. Secondly, we need to give up control and allow God to work in our lives by asking him to guide our steps and direct our thoughts. Finally, we must trust God to work out all these troubles for the good and in his timing.

Is God Really Present?

It is only natural to wonder where God is in the midst of all of our hurt. Even though Jesus specifically states in Matthew 28:20 (ESV), "I am with you always, to the end of the age," we feel as if God has abandoned us. Trusting God is hard when life is not what we expected. Sensing God's presence in the good times is much easier than in the not-so-good times.

The birth of my children has always been a reminder of God's presence in my life. My firstborn child, a son, was born on my husband's birthday, and a few years later we welcomed a daughter, born on my birthday. A geneticist shared with me that the chances of those two blessed events happening as they did were one in a million! Eventually, we looked forward to welcoming a third child into our world. Unfortunately, that pregnancy ended in a miscarriage giving rise to great sadness for our family. Whether it was coincidence, a God-incident, or a Godwink (term coined by author Squire Rushnell), unbelievably, in time, we were blessed with another child who arrived in the very week we had been expecting our unborn child. Was God reminding me that he is always with me, even when I felt he was far away?

My "Birthday Blessings" story continued on through the life of my dear friend. Her husband died suddenly of a heart attack at a young age, leaving her with three young children. The years passed, her children grew up, and one day my friend was blessed with a grandson born on her husband's birthday! Was God reminding my friend that he had been with her through all of the grief she had endured? I don't know for sure, but I do know that God's Word is true, and he has promised to be with us always.

"Letting Go" Considerations

When is it time to think about letting go, at least for the present time? Perhaps you have reached out to your alienator in every way possible through mail, email, text messages, or phone calls. You may have been met with silence, additional reprimands, or even restraining orders. Cards and gifts may not have been acknowledged as received and may even have been returned. No matter what your efforts have been, the rejection just seems to continue on and on. It's then that you may ponder letting go, for now, and putting your life back together. You have done your part, but you realize that reconciliation requires two parties.

If possible, so far as it depends on you, live peaceably with all.

(Romans 12:18 ESV)

The condition of our overall health is an important consideration. Studies show grandparent alienation affects mental, emotional, and physical health. Understandably, grandparents have suffered the loss of their adult child and grandchildren, and they are grieving and feeling stressed. According to Jeffrey Birk, PhD, researcher at Columbia University, "chronic stress is associated with such health issues as muscle tension, digestive problems, headaches, weight gain or loss, trouble sleeping, heart disease, susceptibility to cancer, high blood pressure, and stroke [1]." At some point, taking care of ourselves must become a priority.

Indeed, estrangement has a great impact on the lives of grandparents. Consider how estrangement has impacted your general sense of well-being in the following areas: your identity, happiness, family, friends, relationships, finances, holidays, self-worth, contentment, and spirituality. Have other areas of your life been impacted? Identify some of these areas and begin to ponder the idea of letting go of some of the hurts and heartaches you experience each day.

Traveling the Road of Estrangement

The journey of family estrangement is certainly not the scenic, enjoyable route we had planned to take in our later years. The days are cloudy, our minds are foggy, and the storm of alienation is hitting us with such force that it is hard to make our way forward. We may find ourselves feeling on top of the world when reconciliation appears on the horizon. But, regrettably, we may find ourselves in the valley again when we are shunned and rejected one more time. We feel as if we are being dragged down this path, stuck in the ruts of rumination, by the power our children have over our lives. What do we do?

Becoming cognizant of the fact that the road to grandparenting is closed for now, we may come to accept that we are being rerouted. It's not the path we ever imagined we would be on, but it is our path for now. For a moment, think back to a time you used GPS. Once you entered the destination, did you notice that GPS suggested more than one route to get you to your journey's end? Similarly, while traveling the road of family estrangement, we have alternate detours from which to choose. We can embrace all our hurt, anger, heartache, and sadness as we travel down that rough, rutted, potholed route. Or, we could move our emotional baggage from the front seat, to the back seat, to the trunk, and eventually leave it beside the road, lightening our load for a more peaceful journey. No matter which route you travel, you will arrive at the same destination. Dropping emotional baggage is not easy, but with God as our co-pilot, we can seek to find peace for the present and hope for the future. (Note: The next couple of chapters share some strategies for coping with negative emotions and dropping all that baggage.)

Holding on to Hope for the Future

Even though we know we can't change our adult children or their behaviors, we still want to be loved and respected by them. In our mind, that's what children, no matter how old, ought to do. Thoughts of letting go cause us to feel angst. We fear the loss of relationships with our children and grandchildren, and we feel we have a duty to soldier on and persevere.

For me, the idea of letting go felt a whole lot like giving up. The estrangement was ongoing, and I needed to fix it one way or another, or so I thought. How could I just walk away from my grandkids?

But letting go is a matter of accepting the way things are at the present time. It's acknowledging that we still hurt and at the same time accepting that we have no control over the situation. We can be free to let it go for now. Rob Rienow, author of *Healing Family Relationships* states, "We choose acceptance because we are seeking healing, reconciliation, and transformation. We accept our family member with all their baggage while praying for God to bring transformation to the relationship [2]." Acceptance doesn't mean it will be a forever thing. We can continue to hold on to hope for the future.

We don't know what lies ahead. Everything could turn out to be grand. For now, we have a choice to make—find joy in our lives or remain downhearted.

"A happy heart makes the face cheerful, but heartache crushes the spirit."

(Proverbs 15:13 NIV)

Prayer: *Dear Heavenly Father, thank you for the blessings you have given us. We ask for wisdom, strength, and courage to navigate our family estrangements. We pray that you will heal our broken families. For now, bless us with your peace and continued hope. In Your name we pray, Amen.*

Finding Peace in the Midst of Hurt

―――

Be still and know that I am God.

Psalm 46:10 ESV

When in the midst of challenging situations, it is not uncommon to feel as if our days are continually colored by negative thoughts and emotions brought on by our struggles. While there are no quick fixes, in addition to his constant love and support, God has blessed us with the capacity to work with our thoughts and emotions in intentional ways.

Negativity Bias

Family estrangement causes many of us to feel a continual sense of grief. We can be overwhelmed by what feels like dark shadows of despair and hopelessness engulfing us. Research supports the fact that our brains do indeed have a bias toward negativity. An article by Hara Marano published in *Psychology Today* cites the work of John Cacioppo, PhD, and his efforts to determine why our brains are more inclined to focus on negative thoughts. "The brain, Cacioppo demonstrated, reacts more strongly to stimuli it deems negative, as there is a greater surge in electrical activity. Thus, our attitudes are more heavily influenced by downbeat news than good news [1]." Negativity bias can keep us stuck in a continual cycle of rumination. Attempting to fall asleep at night, as well as focusing on the tasks at hand during the day, become challenging. Our minds continually try to make sense of things and seek out solutions. For the sake of our mental health, we need to be mindful of our negative thinking and take steps to focus on positivity.

How do we rid ourselves of our negative thoughts when they keep swirling around in our head with no hope of settling down? How do we give prominence to the positives and oust the negatives? Following is an account of my feeble attempt to do just that. One day I decided I was tired of feeling gloomy and headed to my favorite nature center to walk my worries away. As I wandered through the woods, I noticed that my steps increased to a faster pace, and my heartbeat became more rapid. I found myself ruminating on the unfairness of being rejected as a grandmother, the sadness of not being able to see my grandchildren, and the intense anger I was experiencing. My negative thoughts showed no signs of abating. They kept zipping along the pathways, which felt more like freeways, in my mind. Undoubtedly, I needed some strategies on how to go about refocusing my thoughts.

Strategies for Staying Present

Fortunately, in recent years, researchers have discovered the concept of neuroplasticity, the brain's ability to form new neural pathways throughout life. Whereas the default mode for our brain is to focus on the negative, it *is* possible for our brain to reorganize and rearrange. In an article published by Harvard, authors Rastegari and Shafer cite some encouraging information from Metta McGarvey, a Harvard lecturer and mindfulness expert. She states, "Our brains can change, physically, as a result of learning. In a process called 'experience dependent neuroplasticity,' neural connections grow based on what we're learning. Repeating the same thoughts, feelings, and behaviors increases synaptic connectivity, strengthens neural networks, and creates new neurons through learning [2]." Amazing! Just recognizing that the brain of a human being has the ability to chase away negative emotions is in itself motivating indeed. With that knowledge, educating ourselves on strategies to help us focus on positive thoughts and create new pathways in our mind becomes the objective.

Intentionality

The first step requires us to make a commitment and become intentional about putting forth our best efforts to let go of our hurt and to find some joy in our lives again. In other words, we need to make a decision to throw off, get away from, and rid ourselves of the pain. It won't be an easy journey, but like one that is analogous to a weight loss journey that requires us to form new habits. It is to be expected that ups and downs will occur along the way, but with dedication and persistence, the end goal can be attained.

Feelings of heartache and hopelessness are still allowed, but we cannot let them consume our day. An elderly man whose wife had passed away provides us with an example of managing grief. Upon arising, his morning routine would include some time sitting in his wife's rocking chair, reading Scripture, looking at pictures, and reflecting on the good times and wonderful memories. After several minutes or so, he would get on with his day. One might surmise that eventually the elderly man spent less and less time in the rocking chair, but his morning observances were a great first step! It may be that setting aside some time each day to acknowledge our hurt is a necessary step. The following strategies for processing negative thoughts may help us move forward.

Journaling

Research has proven over and over again that journaling is therapeutic. I have to say, I had my doubts about the effectiveness of writing. Words don't come easily for me, and the thought of journaling seemed a burdensome task. Reluctantly, I gave it a try and discovered that, indeed, the research was correct. The emotions circling endlessly inside my head were more subdued. I was able to wrap my mind around all the commotion and discern my feelings. *"Yes, that's what's bothering me"* and *"that's why I feel the way I do"* were thoughts I experienced.

The expression of my heartaches and anguish through written words helped me understand my emotions more clearly. Doubts on the value of journaling had been erased.

Staying Present

Another strategy for focusing on the positive is to practice redirecting thoughts to the present moment. Centering attention on the task at hand, such as cleaning the house, planting flowers, playing golf, or baking cookies, keeps our mind from wandering and keeps negative thoughts at bay. This is not an easy endeavor, and it takes practice. Setting a goal of staying present throughout a brief activity that is a part of your daily routine, let's say making a morning cup of coffee, would be a good starting point. The objective is to stay focused and genuinely enjoy making the cup of coffee, not just go through the motions while our mind continues to swirl with gloomy and depressing thoughts. Instead, focus on the distinct aroma of the coffee grounds, the sounds of the coffee maker, the hot steam arising from the cup, the shape of the coffee mug, and finally, the deep rich taste of hot coffee as you slowly sip your special brew. Once you've experienced some success in staying present for a short period of time, try an activity that requires more time.

One day I decided to give this strategy of staying in the present a try by baking my favorite cookies. Employing all of my five senses, with the intention of keeping my mind from wandering, helped me stay focused on the measuring and mixing of the whole wheat flour, sweet maple syrup, crunchy walnuts, rich chocolate chips, and other ingredients to create a batch of delicious homemade cookies. Instead of rushing through the process in an effort to just get done, I thoroughly enjoyed baking the cookies and did not absent-mindedly forget a single ingredient. The goal of savoring the present and forgetting the past, at least for that period of time, was achieved!

Keeping focus on the present moment is not an easy task. The process is somewhat analogous to the game of "Whac-a-Mole." The objective in this famous arcade game is to hit the heads of moles with a mallet as they quickly and randomly pop up. Likewise, staying present requires one to keep random thoughts from popping up and then letting them go when they do. That skill will surely take practice.

Extinguish Negativity, Kindle Positivity

Replacing negative thoughts with positive thoughts is another strategy to employ. As estranged grandparents, we most likely experience the same tiresome and distressing thoughts again and again. We need a plan. Consider some of the anxious thoughts that keep recurring in your mind. For example, you may be feeling devalued as a parent because of the rejection by your adult child. Write that or any specific, constant negative thought you experience on a piece of paper. On the other side, make note of a positive phrase or statement that you can use to replace that negative thought when it surfaces, and thus, redirect your thinking. The positive statement could be a list of ways in which you *were* a wonderful parent. Use your positive statements to replace any negative thoughts that keep resurfacing.

Other Strategies

Spending time in nature, volunteering, and practicing gratitude are other strategies to employ to keep focused on the present. These concepts will be explored in upcoming chapters. In general, be deliberate and intentional about developing a plan, and then practice, practice, practice!

Savor God's Presence and God's Greatness

In an effort to find peace in the midst of our heartbreaking journey, it's essential to remain engaged in the here and now and to recognize God's presence. Psalm 46:10 (ESV) reminds us to "be still and know that I am God." Undoubtedly, a state of quietude is something we desire, but it may seem unattainable when our lives feel so out of control. The broken family relationships, hopelessness, despair, and hurt associated with our estrangement make life seem overwhelming. How *can* we be still?

Just as we can practice savoring our morning cup of coffee and freshly baked cookies, we can ponder God's Word and savor his presence. Take note of these words from the Bible: "God is our refuge and strength, a very *present* help in trouble" (Psalm 46:1 ESV) and "the Lord your God is *in your midst*; he will quiet you by his love" (Zephaniah 3:17 ESV). We can be still because we know that God is indeed present in our lives! With the reassurance that God is listening, spending quiet moments with God is comforting.

In addition to savoring God's presence, take time to savor God's greatness. Ponder his miracles. He created the world, parted the Red Sea, turned water into wine, sent manna from heaven, caused the sun and moon to stand still, and cured the sick and lame, to name a few. By taking time to savor God's power, we come to realize that "nothing will be impossible with God" (Luke 1:36 ESV). We can trust that he is working in our lives.

Prayer: *Dear Heavenly Father, thank you for your promise to be with us always. Even when days are difficult and you seem far away, we trust you are by our side. Your faithfulness gives us hope. Bless us with your peace. In your name we pray, Amen.*

An Attitude of Gratitude

———

Rejoice always, pray without ceasing, give thanks in all circumstances; for this is the will of God in Christ Jesus for you.

1 Thessalonians 5:16-18 ESV

Rejoice always? Give thanks in all circumstances? Seriously? How can one be grateful in the midst of an abundance of hurt? The early days of my estrangement brought great sadness. I felt as if there was a cloud hanging over my head constantly. It wasn't just any cloud, but a dark and ominous cloud that followed me every minute of each day. It was impossible to dismiss the gloomy feelings of rejection and the loss of my identity as a grandmother. Anger and thoughts of how to weather the storm of alienation kept me from falling asleep at night. Truly, the canvas of my life was painted with nothing but dark colors. Frankly, acquiring an attitude of gratitude seemed absolutely impossible.

"Give thanks in all circumstances" ranks right up there with "all have sinned and fall short of the glory of God" (Romans 3:23 ESV) and "forgive seventy-seven times" (Matthew 18:22 ESV) for words in the Bible we do not want to hear. We want to shut our eyes to certain truths and directives. In fact, because feeling grateful is perhaps the furthest thing from your mind right now, you may be thinking about skipping this chapter. However, do take into consideration that one day gratitude can become a valuable tool for coping with and managing the heartache of estrangement.

That being said, God allows us to express our negative emotions and cry out to him. In Psalm 40:1 (NIV) David writes, "I waited patiently for the Lord; he turned to me and heard my cry." God acknowledges our hurts. He comforts us with these words: "Peace I leave you, my peace I give to you. Do not let your hearts be troubled" (John 14:27 NIV). David gives account of God's tender care in Psalm 40:2 (NIV). "He [God] lifted me out of the slimy pit, out of the mud and mire; he set my feet on a rock and gave me a firm place to stand." We can be comforted knowing that we do not need to remain in the pit of hopelessness.

Did you catch that key thought in the words of Psalm 40 in the paragraph above? David waited *patiently*. Likewise, practicing gratitude requires patience. Gratefulness cannot be attained instantaneously. Focusing on goodness, developing an attitude of gratitude, and finding peace in our lives all take time.

Gratitude Defined

The Merriam-Webster dictionary defines gratitude as the state of being grateful: thankfulness. Robert Emmons [1], leading scientific expert on gratitude, defines gratitude as an affirmation of goodness and the recognition that the sources of goodness are outside ourselves. Speaking of sources of goodness, the Bible emphasizes that "every good gift and every perfect gift is from above" (James 1:17 ESV).

Gratitude, a Guiding Light

When life is rolling along and things are going smoothly, we tend to take many of our blessings for granted. But when troubles and heartaches come our way, we suffer in darkness and despair, all while contemplating our misfortunes. Consider the paintings of Thomas Kincade, one of America's most collected artists. The dark colors in Kincade's paintings provide sharp contrast to the bright colors he paints to fully depict light in all of his artwork. Kincade claims, "As a painter, light is the essence of what I try to capture on canvas—a light that dispels darkness, that chases away confusion and despair."

A light that dispels darkness and despair sounds just like something we estranged grandparents need! The practice of gratitude can be that guiding light that disseminates darkness, illuminates good, and leads the way forward.

The Magnitude of an Attitude of Gratitude

After two decades of research, gratitude has been proven to be "one of the most scientifically backed practices in positive psychology [2]." Researchers Wong and Brown concluded from their study that gratitude has the power to "disconnect us from toxic, negative emotions, as well as the rumination that often accompanies them [3]." Thus, it is not surprising that the multitude of studies on gratitude indicate the mental, physical, and emotional benefits are many. Alienated grandparents experiencing the consequences of broken family relationships have much to gain by practicing gratitude. Gratitude has the potential to turn our despair into hope and our heartache into peace, and perhaps even joy!

Studies have proven time and time again that the practice of gratitude (affirming the good), creates a sense of happiness, joy, enthusiasm, willpower, and optimism, as well as a sense of purpose in life. Gratitude improves emotional well-being, lowers levels of anxiety and depression, boosts self-esteem, and strengthens social relationships. Undeniably, life offers us a more positive outlook when viewing it through the prism of gratefulness.

In 1899 Ada Blenkhorn wrote the popular Gospel hymn, *Keep on the Sunny Side*. According to hymntime.com, Blenkhorn was "inspired by her disabled nephew, who always wanted his wheelchair pushed down 'the sunny side' of the street." The inspiring lyrics challenge us to "keep on the sunny side of life and to trust in our Savior who's keepin' everyone in his care." So, keep that tune in your head and perhaps you can add a bit of a spring to your step.

An abundance of research supports the fact that gratitude promotes physical health. Studies indicate that the positive effects of practicing gratitude include the following: improved physical fitness, better eating habits and nutrition, fewer headaches, healthier hearts, improved digestive and respiratory systems, lower blood pressure, stronger immunity, and fewer sleep disturbances. That long list of benefits certainly may inspire one to take action.

The mental, physical, and emotional benefits of gratefulness are amazing and certainly underscore the magnitude of an attitude of gratitude.

A Guide to Gratitude

Learning to manage negative emotions in the midst of estrangement is a challenging task. It's not as though we can just flip a switch from sadness to happiness and all will be well. That being said, it is quite interesting to note that one research study [4] indicates that the practice of gratitude may be able to change and rewire the brain. That is incredible! Perhaps, over time, we can indeed flip those negative thoughts to positive ones. Following are steps one might take to begin the practice of gratitude.

Pray

God does direct us to "give thanks in all circumstances" (1 Thessalonians 5:18 ESV), but take note that God does not direct us to give thanks for all circumstances. Rather, in the midst of our hurt, we can thank God for what we have and then trust God for what we need. We can also ask God for guidance and strength as we embark on the journey of practicing gratitude.

"Devote yourselves to prayer, being watchful and thankful."

(Colossians 4:2 NIV)

Reflect Upon Your Blessings

One spring day I decided to take out a notebook and list some things for which I was grateful. I was exhausted with the continuous rumination of dejectedness and emotional turmoil and needed to try something. I was pleasantly surprised when my list became much longer than I anticipated: wildflowers, ducklings, rain, coffee, walks, good health, music, books, church, friends, neighbors, robins, green trees, sunsets, ponds, the moon, projects, volunteer opportunities, home, technology, hobbies, road trips, new recipes, and laughter! I was heartened that the act of counting my blessings lifted my spirits and helped foster a sense of optimism on my day. Reflect on the following quotes regarding gratitude:

"The heart that gives thanks is a happy one, for we cannot feel thankful and unhappy at the same time." —Douglas Wood

"When one door of happiness closes, another opens; but often we look so long at the closed door that we do not see the one which has been opened for us." —Helen Keller

"We can only be said to be alive in those moments when our hearts are conscious of our treasures." —Thornton Wilder

Be Intentional

It's important to be intentional about practicing gratitude and making it a part of our daily routine. Committing to a plan to chronicle at least three blessings, big ones (such as a wedding) or little ones (such as the sweetness of a strawberry), on a daily basis is a great start. If blessings are documented in a gratitude journal at the end of the day, we can fall asleep counting our blessings! Or, perhaps we might start the day with a cup of coffee and take note of several things for which to be thankful. This approach would help put a bright outlook on the activities we have planned for the day. Consider other options for recording blessings. Index cards and Post-it notes offer good alternatives. Place them on a mirror, the refrigerator, or anywhere around the house as a reminder of all the goodness in your life. Creating a photo gallery of things for which you are grateful offers another option. In addition, our digital world offers online gratitude journals and apps. Those options may appeal to the technologically gifted and are certainly something to explore.

Reframe the Negative

While it makes sense that focusing on the positives in our lives keeps us from wallowing on the negative aspects, how do we handle those never-ending menacing feelings of gloom that just won't go away? One research study [5] by Phillip Watkins provides some insights. Participants were asked to ponder and then write about possible positive outcomes of an unpleasant event that occurred in their lives. From the study, "it appeared that grateful processing allowed participants to see an unpleasant event from their past in a new light with a different perspective." The old adage that it is more desirable to view life as a glass half full, rather than a glass half empty, seems to be validated by this research. Although feelings of downheartedness and despair will resurface, reframing the negative aspects will help drive them away.

Rejoice in Suffering

Rejoice in suffering? Really? That directive seems totally out of the question. How can we be grateful for the pain and sufferings in our lives? Nevertheless, in the book of Romans 5:3-4 (ESV), Paul tells us to "rejoice in our sufferings, knowing that suffering produces endurance, and endurance produces character, and character produces hope." Sufferings provide us with two options: to live our days in agony or to practice patience and endurance. Endurance, or perseverance, is the capability to carry on when we feel like giving up. Endurance, in turn, produces character. And, whereas a strong character helps us navigate the ups and downs of life, it also helps us place our hope in God, trusting him to be with us in the good times and in the not-so-good times.

Repeat, Repeat, Repeat

There is much research on the length of time it takes to form a new habit. Many experts believe 21 days is the minimum requirement. Some follow the 21-90 rule with the philosophy that it takes 21 days to create a habit and 90 days to make it part of one's lifestyle. Some behavioral experts believe it takes months. The consistent theme here is that it takes time to incorporate something new into a daily routine. One might not notice the benefits of the practice of gratitude at first. So, set a goal to complete your journal daily for an extended period of time, and then take note of the positive results—hopefully, a more peace-filled you with an attitude of gratitude!

Prayer: *Dear Heavenly Father, help us give thanks in all circumstances, help us understand the power and magnitude of gratitude, and help us wait patiently as we journey through these troubling times. In your name we pray, Amen.*

Holidays and Special Days

Rejoice in the Lord always. I will say it again: Rejoice!

Philippians 4:4 NIV

Holidays and special days are bittersweet. We try our best to experience the joy of special occasions, but the brokenness of our family is amplified in our alienator's absence. Just when we feel we have begun to make progress in our healing journey, a holiday comes along and feelings of sadness, hopelessness, and loss are reactivated. Rather than looking forward to celebrating, we may find ourselves wishing for these special days to pass quickly. For many estranged grandparents, the pain is inevitable. Acknowledging the fact that we are still hurting is all right. Dealing with holiday heartache will take time. Turn to God, our ever-present help in times of trouble, and ask for strength during these especially difficult days. Then, we need to make the most of each holiday and every special day.

How *do* we survive, let alone find peace or joy in holiday celebrations? Following are some suggestions:

- *Make a plan and follow through*
- *Focus on family and friends who are in your life*
- *Identify what is important to you*
- *Create new traditions and opportunities for happiness*
- *Do something for others*

The above guidelines are short in number, but implementing them will require some time. Gather a pen, paper, a computer, and a calendar. Prepare to do some serious list making, as well as some internet searches. Make lists of family and friends to include in your celebrations. Consider the significance of the holiday and the most important aspects on which you want to focus. Search various websites for some ideas of new traditions and activities, as well as events that are happening in your area. Create a specific plan for the day, put it in writing, and add the events to your calendar. Then, carry out your plan and make some new memories.

Birthdays

It's your special day, and you are holding on to hope that your adult child will remember and give you a call or send a text or email. After all, it's your birthday! If communication occurs, the conversation or message may feel strained and uncomfortable, a further reminder of the family estrangement. If communication does not happen at all, feelings of rejection set in once again. Therefore, it's important to recognize that since we cannot control our adult child's behavior, we should not allow our alienators to rob us of our happiness.

Birthdays are a special celebration of life. It's a reminder of the day you were born and all the years in between then and now. It is a time to thank God for another year of life, to reflect on the past, and to look to the future with optimism. Ecclesiastes 11:8 (ESV) reminds us that "even those who live many years should rejoice in them all." Despite being in the throes of adversity, we ought to celebrate each year of life as a blessing from God.

Because we have been rejected by our children, we may feel worthless and disheartened. The very nature of estrangement causes us to question our value. However, we cannot be defined by our alienators. Take time to ponder your personal worth. Use your journal to create a list of blessings you have received from God and ways in which God has used you to bless others. It is important to take time to build up self-esteem. Check out the Bible verse below to discover why self-regard is so important.

Above all else, guard your heart, for everything you do flows from it.

(Proverbs 4:23 NIV)

If we do not love ourselves, it is impossible to love others. Take time to celebrate you and all the blessings you have received. Consider using your talents to do something for someone else on your special day. Take time to identify what is important to you, make a plan, put it on your calendar, and follow through with intentions to make your day special.

Mother's Day and Father's Day

These two special days honoring parents are quite popular and have interesting histories. Mother's Day was established as an official United States holiday in 1914. It wasn't until 58 years later that Father's Day became a national holiday. It is an interesting fact that more phone calls are made on Mother's Day than any other day of the year, causing phone traffic to spike by as much as 37 percent [1]. Furthermore, on Father's Day, economists estimate that over one billion dollars are spent on gifts [2]. Honoring parents has become paramount in our society, and it is no wonder that estranged grandparents experience heartache and sadness on these special days.

My first Mother's Day as an alienated grandmother was filled with apprehension. I was fairly certain my estranged son would not text or call, but I spent the day secretly hoping he would. When the Mother's Day greeting from my firstborn son never materialized, feelings of rejection resurfaced in my heart, and the state of our fractured relationship was reaffirmed.

We hope our adult children would find it in their hearts to follow the words of the fifth commandment: "Honor your father and your mother" (Exodus 20:12 ESV). We long to feel loved, honored, and respected as parents on these noteworthy days. After all, we have invested so much time and energy in raising and caring for our children, and we love them. We miss our adult children and our grandchildren. We are sad that our grandchildren do not have loving and supportive grandparents in their lives. Despite all the sorrow we face, we cannot permit our adult children to define our value as parents.

Set aside some time to ponder all the ways in which you have been a loving, productive, valuable, and caring parent. Create a list in your journal. Then, develop and make good on a plan to recognize, acknowledge, and celebrate you, a loving parent!

Thanksgiving

Thanksgiving most likely gives rise to images of the perfect family gathering. We envision everyone seated around a beautifully decorated dinner table, the stuffed turkey, the pumpkin pie, and the warm sentiments of just being family. When that image of the ideal Thanksgiving is shattered, we feel heartbroken. We are envious of other families who seem to have it all together. Again, it is acceptable to acknowledge the pain we are feeling, but we must also realize that we can choose to make the most of this potentially stressful day.

Thanksgiving is a great day to take out your gratitude journal or the largest piece of paper you can find. Make a list of every blessing you can imagine. Focus on all the things you do have, and not on the things you don't have. After recounting and chronicling all your blessings, give thanks to God for them.

Oh, give thanks to the Lord, for he is good; for his steadfast love endures forever!

(1 Chronicles 16:34 ESV)

The next task is to create a strategic plan for your Thanksgiving Day. Many churches have services on Thanksgiving Eve and Thanksgiving Day. Then, consider these options that other estranged grandparents have suggested:

- *Cook a turkey and prepare your favorite dishes and desserts*
- *Invite others who are not spending Thanksgiving with family*
- *Make reservations at a place you love to eat*
- *Take a Thanksgiving hike on a nature trail*
- *Volunteer at a homeless shelter or soup kitchen*
- *Ease the loneliness of others by visiting a home for seniors*
- *Prepare a meal for a needy family*
- *Play some board games and watch movies*
- *Participate in a local Turkey Trot for charity*
- *Pray for your family and others facing estrangement*
- *Make new traditions*

It's important to be intentional about your course of action for the day. Make a plan and bring it to completion.

Christmas

Christmas is that very special time of year when all seems merry and bright for everyone but us. The Christmas services, concerts, music, cookie baking, children's programs, decorations, Christmas trees, and gift buying all take on a whole new meaning without our family intact. Sorrow seems to linger over the season, and the star atop the tree appears dimmer. We, as estranged grandparents, can hardly describe

Christmas as the most wonderful time of the year. Furthermore, because Christmas lasts for a season, not just a single day, surviving this holiday is a much greater challenge.

Focusing on the true meaning of Christmas, the gift of Jesus as our Savior, gives us a real reason to find joy.

And the angel said to them, "Fear not, for behold, I bring you good news of great joy that will be for all the people. For unto you is born this day in the city of David a Savior, who is Christ the Lord."

(Luke 2:10-11 ESV)

Even so, not having the opportunity to share the joy of Christmas with our earthly family is nothing less than heartbreaking. It is completely normal to experience feelings of emotional hurt, and it's all right to acknowledge the existence of our pain. We can't let those feelings consume our days. We need to stay in the present and treasure each moment. Our Christmas season will have a new look, and purposeful planning is a necessity. Consider old traditions, new traditions, volunteer opportunities, ways to share Christmas with others, church services, special concerts, and events in your area. Take out the calendar for the month of December and fill it with activities that will provide focus and meaning for the Christmas season.

Plan, Plan, Plan

The word "plan" seems to be the recurring theme for surviving holidays and special days. Planning provides us with the motivation to focus on what we've identified as priorities for the day. Plans give clarity to our thoughts and actions and set forth a timeline for us to follow on those difficult days. Plans give purpose to our celebrations.

Rejoice in the Lord always. I will say it again: Rejoice!

(Psalm 118:24 ESV)

Prayer: *Dear Heavenly Father, we thank you that your love for us never ends and your compassions never fail. When suffering is present in our lives, we pray that you will lift our feelings of sadness and fill our hearts with hope. Guide us in our journey of life as we seek peace for the present and hope for the future. In your name we pray, Amen.*

Memories and Legacies

———

So now faith, hope, and love abide, these three; but the greatest of these is love.

1 Corinthians 13:13 ESV

M emory boxes, memory books, and photo books provide a connection to past generations and give children and grandchildren a sense of belonging and identity as they learn about their family history and roots. Furthermore, author and financial planner Wes Moss shares the thought that "when grandparents offer stories and memories with family members and other loved ones, it helps these listeners to grow in their own lives [1]." Stories of the past provide opportunities to learn valuable lessons, family values, and faith.

Content Ideas

So, what do grandchildren want to know about their grandparents? Ancestry.com conducted a survey [2] and found that grandchildren want to hear stories about when their grandparents were young, their childhood memories, their heritage, and their advice about life. Written narratives and stories, video recordings, sound recordings, and photos can all be utilized by grandparents to share their lives with their grandchildren. Possible topics to address might include favorite games, school days, pets, holidays, traditions, travels, happy times, faith, wisdom gained from life's experiences, feelings, and really anything you want them to know.

Consider including books, souvenirs, personal notes, and special items. For example, while walking along the beach, I discovered some beautiful seashells and stopped to collect a few for my grandchildren. The golden colored shells were for my grandchild with blond hair, the unusual looking ones were for my grandchild with a sense of humor, and the smallest seashells were designated for my youngest grandchild. I decided to add them to their memory boxes so that one day each of them would know I was thinking of them during the years we couldn't be together.

Compiling the photos, special items, and the words that you want to place on the hearts of your children and grandchildren is a major undertaking. A good amount of time will be required to complete this project, for sure.

Photo Books

In an article written for GrandKidsMatter, poet Carolyn Scully states that "photographs are doorways to memories that invite stories to be told and connections between generations to be made [3]." You may have more photos than you need, so you will have to do some organizing. Sort through the pictures and organize them chronologically or by theme, such as holidays, vacations, family, and so on. Choose a special album or photo box for each grandchild. Begin by writing the reasons why you assembled the photo collection. Include personal messages to each grandchild, and write captions or stories to accompany the photos. You might consider using a digital format. It is also possible to upload your photos to certain websites, and a book can be created and printed for you.

Sense of Hope

Has "clean the basement" or "organize the file cabinet" ever been on your to-do list? If you are like me, those daunting tasks can seem overwhelming and usually get moved to a later date. The creation of memories and legacies for our children and grandchildren is also a project that can easily be shelved. Personally, I found myself procrastinating day after day and week after week. But, eventually, I settled on a plan to create memory boxes, one for each grandchild, filled with photos and mementos. I discovered that the time spent gathering and organizing the pictures and special items did indeed dull my heartache and lessen the pain of estrangement. Even though I could not connect with my grandchildren at that time, thoughts of having opportunities in the future to regain the years we had lost gave me a sense of hope. Perhaps the creation of memory books, memory boxes, and photo books will be a source of comfort to you also.

Prayer: *Dear Heavenly Father, we ask that you draw our children and grandchildren into a relationship with you. In whatever way possible, we pray that our faith in you and our love for them will be evident. Help us share a legacy of love. In your name we pray, Amen.*

Walking Forward with Hope

———

May the Lord cause you to flourish.

Psalm 115:14 NIV

We long for the days when our family was altogether and whole. It is not uncommon to engage in the act of reminiscing. According to the Oxford dictionary, reminiscing is "indulging in enjoyable recollection of past events." It is thinking about and sharing memories of a childhood home, school days, celebrations, friends, or unforgettable events from days gone by. Reminiscing generates happy memories and cheerful thoughts. Recollecting the "good old days" reminds us that joy once existed in our lives, and it may give rise to a yearning for the past—for happier days. For Jesus' disciples, they probably remembered the days of old when Jesus was with them on earth. For us, we remember untroubled times with our loved ones. But reminiscing can get us stuck-stuck in thinking our lives are filled with despair and hopelessness. Nonetheless, as estranged grandparents we can employ a number of strategies and tools to help us get "unstuck" and move toward finding peace and joy both now and in the future.

Acknowledge the Hurt

"Shake it off. Get over it." Perhaps these are words of advice you have heard from a well-meaning friend or relative. I recall a time that I shared a particular emotional hurt inflicted by my alienator with some of my family members. My feelings were not validated, and I was frustrated with the lack of empathy. I believe they didn't intend to be unsympathetic; they just didn't want me or them to experience the hurt. As much as we would like to, we can't just wish the heartaches away or pretend they do not exist. It's all right, and even healthy, to take time to acknowledge and process the emotional hurts we have experienced.

How can we move forward? How can we even think about being happy in the midst of all the sadness in our family? How can we even consider giving up on our adult children and grandchildren? We find ourselves feeling guilty about striving to find joy in our lives again, rather than continuing to grieve. Recall from a previous chapter that moving forward does not mean that we forget about and give up on our adult children and grandchildren. We are just accepting that this is the way things are right now. Both heartache and happiness are a part of living. Managing our heartaches will help us focus on the future with hopefulness.

A Plan for Walking Forward

Moving forward requires a commitment on our part to care for ourselves. We can center ourselves on happiness, or we can choose to make heartache the mainstay of our lives. What do we have to gain if we remain in a state of suffering? Our days will be filled with ruminations of negative emotions, silent protests of the unfairness of being rejected, and hopelessness. We cannot hold these hurts so close that we are unable to let go of them. Allowing our alienators to define and control our lives cannot be an option. Acknowledging that it is indeed possible for us to carry on with our lives must be considered. It will necessitate hard work and valiant efforts on our part. Intentional goal setting and planning will be necessary.

Where do we begin? There is no road map for this journey of estrangement. It's not possible to quickly make a U-turn and leave all our hurts behind. The following sections will provide some direction and suggestions for traversing the bumpy road of family alienation and estrangement.

Pray

When my estrangement situation became a reality, and I no longer had contact with my grandkids, I turned to God. I prayed that God would ease the terrible pain and heartache and that our family would be restored. However, I also turned to my own tactics. I read books, sought advice from friends, consulted therapists, reached out, remained silent, and apologized. I tried everything. My family was broken, and I was determined to patch it up and make it whole again! I worked myself into a frenzy trying to do so. All my efforts had failed. I needed a huge reminder that I am not in control and to put my trust in God. I believe this scenario is so true for many of us. We want to take charge and handle it all. Instead, we need to have faith that God is listening when we pray and that he will guide us and work things out in his timing.

Honestly, there are times when our words of prayer seem inadequate. There are times when our emotions take over, and we don't know what to pray for. The initial shock of rejection may render us speechless. Other occasions, such as the death of a loved one, an unexpected event, or an unsettling circumstance, may also leave us with the inability to find the appropriate words to express our petitions to God. It's during these times of weakness that the Holy Spirit steps in and becomes our Helper. The words of Scripture found in Romans 8:26 (ESV) verify this truth: "For we do not know what to pray for as we ought, but the spirit himself intercedes for us with groanings too deep for words." How comforting to know that the Holy Spirit is always with us and in us. We are not alone in times of trouble.

Remain Rooted in the Word of God

If you think about it, raising a family and tending a flower garden share some similarities. As parents, we nurtured our children from infancy to adulthood, beamed with pride at their accomplishments, and were absolutely elated as they married and blessed us with grandchildren! After all, "grandchildren are the crown of the aged" (Proverbs 17:6 ESV). Homeowners and gardeners have most likely had the opportunity to plant flower seeds or young plants, water them, fertilize them, and watch them bloom into a splash of vibrant colors. Undoubtedly, we are in agreement that both flower gardens and families are amazingly beautiful—until they are torn apart!

A family broken by estrangement is not as "pretty as a picture" anymore. The rejection, hurtful words, and despair all take their toll. Likewise, a garden of wilted impatiens, limp begonias, and uprooted coral bells caused by the scorching sun, lack of rain, and hungry critters is not exactly a planter's pride. Shattered dreams and disappointments seem to be the result of all our efforts.

Then, how ironic is it that one day we spot a bright yellow dandelion standing tall and strong somewhere in our yard. How is it that these resilient weeds prosper in the harshest of environments? There are a number of reasons. First of all, the main root of a dandelion can reach a depth of six to 18 inches and is able to pull in nutrients from the soil to sustain itself. In addition, the grooved leaves effectively funnel water directly to the taproot. Dandelions survive and thrive in tough conditions, and we can too if we remain rooted in God's Word.

God speaks to us directly through his Word. The Bible, the written Word of God, shares the wonderful messages of love and hope for all people. The Bible is a "steadfast anchor of the soul" (Hebrews 6:18 ESV) and a "light shining in a dark place" (2 Peter 1:19 NIV). Nancy Guthrie, author of *The One Year Book of HOPE,* counsels us not to underestimate the power of God's Word with this thought: "God's Word can create something good out of the chaos of your circumstances; his Word can still the storm that rages in your heart; his Word can bring healing to your deepest hurts [1]."

Finally, consider these words from Isaiah 58:11 (ESV): "And the Lord will guide you continually and satisfy your desire in scorched places and make your bones strong; and you shall be like a watered garden, like a spring of water, whose waters do not fail." How comforting to know that in our weakness, when our hopes have dried up and withered away, God has not forgotten us. He promises to continually guide us, refresh us, and bless us with his love.

May the Lord cause you to flourish.

(Psalm 115:14 NIV)

Ponder What God Has Done

Consider the meditations of the psalmist who wrote, "I will remember the deeds of the Lord; yes, I will remember your wonders of old" (Psalm 77:11 ESV). Reflecting on all the miraculous things God has done in the past gives way to hope for the future. God demonstrated his power and his love for his people through miracles of the past. Surely the God who turned water into wine, calmed a storm, and healed a blind man is able to work in our lives today. When we ponder God's greatness and his grace, we can hang on to hope.

Learn Something New

Mastering new skills and acquiring new knowledge is beneficial for anyone, including older adults. Cooking, technology, fitness, piano, photography, or other classes of interest can bring renewed joy and happiness to our lives. Learning a new skill such as pickleball or painting within a social setting creates opportunities to connect with others and form new relationships. Learning also creates new neural connections in the brain and improves cognition and memory. One study indicates there is "a clear association between continuous participation in the specific form of lifelong learning courses and the psychological wellbeing of older adults [2]." Another study [3] on the impact of lifelong learning on emotional resilience reported an increase in the ability to cope with stressful situations, as well as a renewed sense of purpose and hope. Take time to consider something you might be interested in learning. Explore the opportunities you have available in your area. Make note in your journal of a few educational topics that catch your eye and follow through on the enrollment process.

Volunteer

Giving our time and talents to others not only makes a difference in their lives, but also in ours. Research demonstrates that the benefits of volunteering include reduced stress, increased happiness, and greater confidence and self-esteem. Studies also indicate that "devoting time to a cause can give us a sense of purpose and take our minds off our troubles [4]." And, by serving others, we are serving God.

"As each has received a gift, use it to serve one another."

(1 Peter 4:10 ESV)

The opportunities are endless, but here are a few possibilities to consider: community gardens, meal programs, nature centers, churches, community clean-ups, food banks, animal shelters, literacy programs, hospitals, and soup kitchens. Check out local school districts for mentoring and tutoring positions. Assisting a neighbor and teaching a class are other options. Search the internet for additional possibilities. Then, make note of anything that sparks your interest and contact the organizations for information on how to get involved.

Enjoy Nature

Many people have conveyed the importance of spending time in nature. John Muir, best known as the father of our national park system, stated that "in every walk with nature one receives far more than he seeks." Anne Frank, a Jewish victim of the Holocaust who kept a diary while in hiding from the Nazis, wrote, "I firmly believe that nature brings solace in all troubles." In addition, much research has been conducted on the effects nature has on human wellbeing. The evidence clearly indicates that the effects are positive. Benefits include increased happiness, reduced stress, and a sense of purpose in life. One study found that "repetitive thought focused on negative emotions, decreased among participants who walked in nature [5]."

That being said, you may recall that my first attempt to get away from all my negative emotions by spending time amongst trees and wildlife was not all that successful. I had worked my way through the woodland and found that my footsteps, my heartbeat, and my mind were all operating at a faster pace than when I first ventured out on the trails. I emerged from the woods in a state of animosity, rather than a state of tranquility. It wasn't until I learned about the magnitude of an attitude of gratitude, as well as how to stay present, that I experienced a sense of peace while strolling through the woods. I discovered that I could focus on the crunching of leaves under my feet, the song of bullfrogs, moss growing on the side of a tree, the unique shapes of leaves, lovely wildflowers, scurrying chipmunks, bright red clumps of berries, and sunshine filtering through the leaves. Needless to say, a walk with Mother Nature is not an instant cure. But with practice and patience, in time, you may find the following quote from Henry David Thoreau to be true:

"I took a walk in the woods and came out taller than the trees."

Play

"We are never more fully alive, more completely ourselves, or more deeply engrossed in anything than when we are playing," writes psychologist Charles Schaefer. Author Lucia Capocchione affirms that concept with the following statement:

"Play keeps us vital and alive. It gives us an enthusiasm for life that is irreplaceable. Without it, life just doesn't taste good."

Participation in play activities keeps us in the present and helps us focus on something enjoyable. Research provides evidence that play activities build our sense of self-worth, increase happiness, lift our mood, and improve mental health by reducing stress, depression, and anxiety. Hopefully, those beliefs on the power of play will motivate us to engage more regularly in some of our favorite activities, as well as inspire us to explore some new options. Categories to consider include: outdoor activities, educational opportunities, music, art, dance class, athletics, sports, theater, get-togethers, vacations, traditional games, gardening, and outings. Take time to research opportunities available in your area. Create a list of your current activities and add some new ones you find interesting. Then, set some dates and follow through on a plan.

Exercise

It is a known fact that exercise is beneficial to our physical health, but current research indicates that physical exercise is instrumental in promoting mental health as well. Researchers are discovering that "physical activity stimulates many brain chemicals that may leave you feeling happier, more relaxed, and less anxious [6]." Numerous studies have shown that feelings of depression, anxiety, and stress decrease when an exercise routine is incorporated into a person's daily activities. Set some realistic goals and then add the plan to your calendar.

Prepare a Purposeful Plan for your Life

We can spend our days feeling heartsick and despondent, or we can think about our future and develop a plan focused on a renewed purpose for our lives. To begin, create a vision statement for your life. Pastor Andy Stanley, author of *Visioneering, Your Guide for Discovering and Maintaining Personal Vision,* shares some thoughts on the interpretation of the word vision. He writes, "Vision brings your world into focus. Vision brings order to chaos. A clear vision enables you to see everything differently [7]."

Think about your purpose. How can you use your gifts, talents, and abilities to create a meaningful life? How can you use your gifts, talents, and abilities to impact others? What are your short and long term goals? Take time to visualize your future and develop a written plan that includes the steps you need to take in order to reach your goals.

Vision statements provide direction for our lives and serve as a road map on our journey of grandparent estrangement. We discover a sense of purpose, and we find that we are a bit more motivated to get up each morning and carry out the plan for the day.

The Journey

Reflecting on the Past

Before focusing on the present and the future, it's important to put the past in perspective. It is probable that you feel you have done everything possible to reconnect with your adult child. You may have come to the realization that you cannot control or change your adult child. Reluctantly, you may have determined that your situation is not fixable at this time and that you cannot continue to remain in the miry bog of despair, anger, and frustration. Isaiah addressed Israel regarding the concept of living in the past and wrote these words: "Forget the former things; do not dwell on the past. See, I am doing a new thing. Now it springs up; do you not perceive it? I am making a way in the wilderness and streams in the wasteland" (Isaiah 43:18-19 NIV). The rejection and heartaches of the past cannot define us and keep a grip on our lives. We need to follow the counsel of Isaiah, not dwell on the past, and trust that God will bless us with a new path forward.

Finding Peace for the Present

Many grandparents have expressed how difficult it is to understand how and why estrangement could have happened in their family. Indeed, the alienation seems incomprehensible and heartbreaking. We cannot expect that the negative emotions we experienced as a result of our broken family will dissipate quickly. Finding peace in our lives requires commitment, intentionality, discipline, and hard work. It is essential to employ the tools and strategies presented in previous chapters to stay in the present. Setbacks will happen, so patience is paramount. We can ask God to guide our journey, and we can continue to pray for our adult children and grandchildren.

In my own journey of estrangement, I prayed daily for God to soften my daughter-in-law's heart and to heal the hurts that caused such anger toward me. Prayers that my grandchildren would be happy and healthy and use their God-given gifts to the best of their abilities were my petitions. Prayers that God would diffuse my anger ascended. I wanted my heart to be in a better place if and when reconciliation would occur.

This is the day that the Lord has made; let us rejoice and be glad in it.

(Psalm 118:24 ESV)

Maintaining Hope for the Future

We don't really know what each new day will bring. Consider these words from Lamentations 3:22-23 (NIV): "Because of the Lord's great love we are not consumed, for his compassions never fail. They are new every morning; great is your faithfulness." God's promises *are* new every morning, and we really don't know what surprises are coming our way.

A few years after my estrangement began, the door to reconciliation opened slightly. My daughter-in-law, much to my surprise, suggested that our family gather for lunch at a local restaurant. The door opened even wider after that initial meeting. I was extremely cautious about renewing our strained relationship. I wondered if my daughter-in-law just needed something from me or if she really wanted to reconcile. Happily, the door opened even wider, and relations have been restored for the most part. There has been no mention of the estrangement years by my daughter-in-law or by me. We have just moved forward. Each family situation is different. If apologies and forgiveness are a part of the reconciliation process for you, that would be a great blessing! If not now, perhaps that conversation will be a part of the future.

One alienated grandmother reported that she unexpectedly received a text message from her daughter after several years of estrangement. Her daughter proposed that they converse again on a monthly basis. Eventually, the conversations increased in frequency, and after some time, the talks led to a reunion. What a blessing!

Hopefully, one day, out of the blue, you will receive a text message, email, phone call, or letter from your adult child that will serve as a stepping stone from estrangement to a loving reconciliation. Until then, always hold on to hope. The following inspirational words from Robert H. Schuller, American pastor, author, and motivational speaker, offer some counsel: "Let your hopes, not your hurts, shape your future." And, in the words of Martin Luther King Jr., "If you lose hope, somehow you lose the vitality that keeps life moving, you lose that courage to be, that quality that helps you go on in spite of it all. And so today I still have a dream." And, for us, we can say that our greatest hope is in the Lord!

But those who hope in the Lord will renew their strength. They will soar on wings like eagles; they will run and not grow weary.

(Isaiah 40:31 NIV)

Summary of Strategies and Tools

We have explored a number of strategies to find peace in the midst of our journey of estrangement. It's difficult to remember them all and implement them in our lives. Following is a summary of the tools we explored. Review the list and choose one or more actions that you can incorporate into your life as you begin your journey to find peace for the present.

Find Peace for the Present

Pray
Read the Bible
Remember What God has Done
Believe you are a Child of God
Learn new Things
Stay in the Present
Turn Negatives into Positives
Practice Gratitude
Set Daily Goals
Forgive
Set Boundaries in Love
Take Care of Yourself
Develop Your Gifts and Talents
Volunteer
Enjoy Nature
Play and Exercise
Create Memory Boxes and Photo Books
Create a Vision for Your Life
Hold on to Hope

Prayer

Heavenly Father,

Thank you for showering us with

your compassion and your love.

We boldly ask that you heal our families

and restore our broken relationships.

Bless us with a sense of peace

through this season of estrangement

and give us hope for the future. Amen.

———————————

May the God of HOPE fill you with all joy and PEACE as you trust in him, so that you may overflow with HOPE by the power of the Holy Spirit.

(Romans 15:13 NIV)

Conversation Road Map

―――

Chapter One: Weathering the Storms of Life

1. Bewilderment describes the state of many alienated parents and grandparents. The words "I don't understand" are spoken over and over again. What is bewildering to you in your family situation?
2. Discovering the "why" will not change our estrangement situation, but exploring possible causes may help us name the problem, identify what we need to forgive, and lift the burden of guilt off our shoulders. Can you relate to any of the causes of grandparent alienation mentioned in this chapter: individualism, cultural emphasis on happiness, growing economic insecurity, change in family values, influential adversaries, mental health concerns, and adult children's perception that parents are obstacles to personal growth?
3. Galatians 6:2 (ESV) challenges us to "bear one another's burdens." In an effort to lighten each other's burdens and offer support, take time to share your story with others in the group.
4. Currently, where do you feel you are on your journey of family estrangement?

Chapter Two: Uncover and Recover

1. According to the research presented in this chapter, withdrawing and suppressing thoughts and feelings can be

harmful to one's physical and mental health. Rather than keeping negative emotions bottled up inside, it is beneficial to share them. Share the feelings and emotions you have experienced as a result of your family estrangement. Did you notice any commonalities within your group?

2. The journaling process gives voice to our pain and helps us manage the hurt. Take a few minutes to write down a few aspects of your family situation that are most concerning to you. Share your thoughts with the group.

3. While on the journey of estrangement, many feel that God is far away. But Jesus tells us he is always by our side. How does God feel distant at this time? How have you sensed the presence of God in your life?

4. God causes all things to work together for the good of those who have been called according to his purpose. These words from Romans 8:28 give us a sense of hopefulness. Can you think of a time in your life, or someone else's life, where something good came out of a bad situation?

Chapter Three: Forgiveness

1. Most estranged parents and grandparents feel they have been wronged and are waiting for an apology from their alienators. What are some reasons given in this chapter for offering forgiveness even though apologies have not been received?

2. What are some stumbling blocks that keep us from considering forgiveness?

3. The words of Maya Angelou, "every great journey starts with a single step," suggest that forgiveness is not an endeavor that can be accomplished quickly. What is a first step you might take to begin the process of forgiveness?

Chapter Four: Reconciliation

1. T.D. Jakes offered some insight as to why our alienators have rejected us. He stated that most people are so focused on their own crises and needs that they seem oblivious to what their actions have done to us. Can you give an example of how this might be true in your family?

2. How would you categorize the state of your heart? Hostile? Sympathetic? Neutral? Forgiving? Other?

3. Many estranged grandparents are in a state of uncertainty when it comes to contacting their adult children. Have you tried to reach out to your adult child to communicate in some way? If so, how? What were the results?

4. Have you been able to have an in-person talk with your adult child? If so, how did you prepare for it? What were the results?

5. In regards to amends letters, experts have varying opinions on their effectiveness. Have you drafted an amends letter to your adult child? If so, how did you go about writing it? Did you follow through with sending it? What were the results?

Chapter Five: Setting Boundaries in Love

1. When estranged parents and grandparents are accused of crossing boundaries, a state of confusion sets in. We may not have heard the term boundaries used in that context before. Have you experienced this new meaning of boundaries?

2. As estranged grandparents, we may be suffering from ongoing verbal abuse, attacks on our character, or unending requests for financial assistance. How might our lives be different if we establish boundaries for ourselves? Why might we be reluctant to set boundaries? At what point do we need to set

guidelines with our estranged family members? Would setting boundaries be beneficial to our alienators?

3. Determine if it is time for you to set boundaries. Use the format outlined in this chapter to write a boundary you feel you need to set. Then ask your group to review it and provide feedback.

Chapter Six: Family Dynamics

1. How has alienation affected other members in your family and extended family?

2. If you shared your story with others in your family, what were their reactions?

3. What problems do you feel others experience when communicating with you knowing that you and your family are struggling with estrangement?

4. Have family members given you advice? If so, what counsel have you received?

5. What specific steps can you take to move forward as a family for now?

6. As you reach out to God, your Repairer, Rebuilder, and Redeemer, what Bible verses come to mind?

Chapter Seven: Letting Go and Letting God

1. In your specific situation, what do you need to let go of and what do you need to let God do?

2. In the Bible we read, "If possible, so far as it depends on you, live peaceably with all" (Romans 12:18 ESV). What meaning does this verse hold for you?

3. There is no way around it. Letting go feels a whole lot like giving up. Talk about the struggles of letting go for now,

while still maintaining hope for the future.

Chapter Eight: Finding Peace in the Midst of Hurt

1. Share examples of how and when your mind tends to default to the negative mode.
2. One strategy for focusing on the positive is to practice redirecting one's thoughts to the present moment. Brainstorm activities you could use to begin working on this approach. Consider projects, hobbies, pastimes, or any daily activity you could employ to practice giving full attention to the task at hand.
3. Replacing negative thoughts with positive thoughts when they occur is another strategy. As a group, identify and write down some of the upsetting and distressing thoughts that tend to resurface in your mind again and again. Then, as a team, write positive phrases or statements to replace the negative thoughts.

Chapter Nine: An Attitude of Gratitude

1. Based on the information in this chapter, create a specific plan for developing an attitude of gratitude in your life.

Chapter Ten: Holidays and Special Days

1. As a group, take on the role of event planners. Brainstorm and create specific plans for upcoming holidays and special days. Consider participation in volunteer opportunities. Perhaps your group could organize a special event or activity

for others.

Chapter Eleven: Memories and Legacies

1. What stories, memories, and thoughts do you want to share with your children and grandchildren?
2. The creation of memories and legacies is an extensive endeavor. Identify the first step you might take and then create a plan for completion.

Chapter Twelve: Walking Forward with Hope

1. Review the list of strategies and tools found under the heading "Find Peace for the Present." Share one or more actions that you plan to incorporate into your life as you begin your journey to find peace for the present.

Next Steps

Even though your group has completed the book, consider a plan to continue meeting on a regular basis for the purpose of discussing setbacks, successes, and sharing what is on your hearts and minds. Form a new group to offer support to other parents and grandparents who are also on the journey of family alienation and estrangement.

Notes

Chapter One: Weathering the Storms of Life

1. Coleman, Joshua. *Rules of Estrangement: Why Adult Children Cut Ties & How to Heal the Conflict.* Harmony Books, 2020.
2. Carr, Kristen. "Giving Voice to the Silence of Family Estrangement: Comparing Reasons of Estranged Parents and Adult Children in a Non-matched Sample." *University of Nebraska-Lincoln Digital Commons*, Amanda J. Holman, Jenna Abetz, Jody Koenig Kellas and Elizabeth Vagnoni. Published in *Journal of Family Communication,* 15: 2015 DOI: 10.1080/15267431.2015.1013106.
3. Grabmeier, Jeff. "Study Examines What Makes Adult Children Cut Ties with Parents." *Ohio State News,* 6 Oct. 2021. OSU.EDU.
4. Ibid.
5. Ibid.
6. Coleman, Joshua. *"Rules of Estrangement: Why Adult Children Cut Ties & How to Heal the Conflict."* Harmony books, 2020.
7. Carr, Kristen. "Giving Voice to the Silence of Family Estrangement: Comparing Reasons of Estranged Parents and Adult Children in a Non-matched Sample." *University of Nebraska-Lincoln Digital Commons*, Amanda J. Holman, Jenna Abetz, Jody Koenig Kellas and Elizabeth Vagnoni. Published in *Journal of Family Communication,* 15:2015

DOI: 10.1080/15267431.2015.1013106.

Chapter Two: Uncover and Recover

1. Vingerhoets, Guy. "Our Emotional Brains: Both Sides Process the Language of Feelings, With the Left Side Labeling the 'What' and the Right Side the "How." *Neuropsychology,* American Psychological Association (apa.org), January 2003.
2. Rodriguez, Tori. "Negative Emotions Are Key to Well-Being." *Scientific American Mind,* 1 May 2013.
3. Hendel, Hilary Jacobs. "Ignoring Your Emotions is Bad for Your Health." *TIME,* 27 Feb. 2018.
4. Watson, Renee L. "Journaling for Mental Health." *University of Rochester Medical Center, Health Encyclopedia,* Marianne Fraser and Paul Ballas, 2023.

Chapter Three: Forgiveness

1. T. D. Jakes Quotes. BrainyQuote.com. BrainyMedia Inc, 2024. 18 July 2024.

Chapter Four: Reconciliation

1. Jakes, T.D. *Let It Go (Forgive So You Can Be Forgiven).* Atria Books, 2012.
2. McGregor, Sheri. *Done With the Crying (Help and Healing for Mothers of Estranged Adult Children).* Sowing Creek Press, 2016.
3. Coleman, Joshua. *Rules of Estrangement: Why Adult children Cut Ties & How to Heal the Conflict.* Harmony Books, 2020.

4. Jantz, Gregory. *How to Deal with Toxic People.* Aspire Press, 2021.
5. Focus on the Family. "*Healing Parent and Adult Child Relationships (Part 1)-Dr. John Townsend.*" [Video]. 23 Nov. 2021, You Tube.

Chapter Five: Setting Boundaries in Love

1. Freeman, Don. *Corduroy.* United States: Viking Press, 1968.
2. Silverstein, Shel. *The Giving Tree.* Harper Collins Publishers, 1964.
3. Fishbein, Rebecca. "Everyone is setting boundaries. Do they even know what it means?" *The Washington Post,* 8 Sept. 2023.

Chapter Six: Family Dynamics

1. Rittenour, Christine. "Communication Surrounding Estrangement: Stereotypes, Attitudes and (Non) Accommodation Strategies." *MDPI,* Stephen Kromka, Sara Pitts, Margaret Thorwart, Janell Vickers, and Kaitlyn Whyte, 20 Oct. 2018, www.mdpi.com/2076-328X/8/10/96.
2. Rodriguez, Tori. "Negative Emotions Are Key to Well-Being." *Scientific American Mind,* 1 May 2013.
3. Smith, Kathleen. "Understanding the Heartbreak of Family Estrangement." *Psycom,* Dina Cagliosto (Medical Reviewer), 5 Oct. 2022.

Chapter Seven: Letting Go and Letting God

1. Birk, Jeffrey. "Chronic Stress Can Hurt Your Overall Health."

Columbia University Irving Medical Center, 19 May 2023.

2. Rienow, Rob. *Healing Family Relationships.* Bethany House, 2020.

Chapter Eight: Finding Peace in the Midst of Hurt

1. Marano, Hara Estroff. "Our Brain's Negative Bias." *Psychology Today,* 20 June 2023.
2. Rastegari, Iman and Leah Shafer. "The Biology of Positive Habits." *Harvard Graduate School of Education,* 21 March 2016.

Chapter Nine: An Attitude of Gratitude

1. Emmons, Robert and Smith, Jeremy Adam. "What Gratitude is and Why it Matters." *The Gratitude Project.* Oakland: New Harbinger Publications, Inc., 2020. 6.
2. Wong, Joel and Joshua Brown, Christina Armenta, Sonja Lyubomirsky, Summer Allen, Amie Gordon, and Kira Newman. "Why Gratitude Is Good for Us." *The Gratitude Project.* Oakland, New Harbinger Publications, Inc., 2020. 52.
3. Wong, J. & Brown, J. (2017 June 6). "How Gratitude Changes You and Your Brain." *Greater Good Magazine,* 21 May 2019.
4. Kini, P. J. Wong, S. McInnis, N.T. Gabana, and J.W. Brown. "The Effects of Gratitude Expression on Neural Activity." NeuroImage 128 (2016): 1-10. *The Gratitude Project.* Oakland: New Harbinger Publications, Inc., 2020. 29.
5. Watkins, Philip and Cruz, Lilia & Holben, Heather and

Kolts, Russell. "Taking Care of Business? Grateful Processing of Unpleasant Memories." *The Journal of Positive Psychology*. 3. 87-89. 2008, 10.1080/17439760701760567.

Chapter Ten: Holidays and Special Days

1. Onion, Amanda, Missy Sullivan, Matt Mullen and Christian Zapata (History.com editors). "Mother's Day 2023." *History.com,* 12 May 2023.
2. Onion, Amanda, Missy Sullivan, Matt Mullen and Christian Zapata (History.com editors). "Father's Day 2023." *History.com,* 15 May 2023.

Chapter Eleven: Memories and Legacies

1. Moss, Wes. "What Grandchildren Really Want to Know About Their Grandparents." *Wes Moss,* 20 Sept. 2019.
2. Ibid.
3. Scully, Carolyn J. "Use Photos to Share Memories with Your Grandkids." *Grandkids Matter,* 4 Nov. 2021.

Chapter Twelve: Walking Forward with Hope

1. Guthrie, Nancy. The One Year Book of Hope. Tynsdale House Publishers, Inc., 2005.
2. Narushima M, Liu J, Diestelkamp N. "Lifelong Learning in Active Ageing Discourse: Its Conserving Effect on Wellbeing, Health and Vulnerability." *Ageing Soc.* 2018 Apr; 38(4):651-675. DOI: 10.1017/S0144686X16001136. Epub 2016 Nov 21. PMID: 29551843; PMCID: PMC5848758.

3. Hammond, Cathie. "Impacts of Lifelong Learning upon Emotional Resilience, Psychological and Mental Health: Fieldwork Evidence." *Oxford Review of Education*, vol. 30, no. 4, 2004, pp. 551–68. JSTOR, www.jstor.org/stable/4127165. Accessed 26 July, 2023.

4. Lockard, Trish. "How Volunteering Improves Mental Health." *National Alliance on Mental Illness* (NAMI), 2 Feb. 2022.

5. Jordan, Rob. "Stanford Researchers Find Mental Health Prescription: Nature." *Stanford News*, 30 June 2015.

6. Mayo Clinic Staff. "Exercise: 7 Benefits of Regular Physical Activity." 26 August 2023.

7. Stanley, Andy. *Visioneering (Your Guide for Discovering and Maintaining Personal Vision)*. Multnomah, 2016.

About the Author

Carolyn is a wife, mother, grandmother, and retired teacher. She has a Bachelor's Degree in Education and a Master's Degree in Reading.She taught for 35 years in both public and parochial schools. Over the years Carolyn has spent much time teaching and coordinating children's minstry programs. Upon becoming an estranged mother and grandmother, her life changed course. Instead of focusing on best practices for teaching reading and connecting children to Jesus, Carolyn gave full attention to navigating the heartbreaking journey of family alienation and estrangement. She launched a support group at her church and wrote a faith-based workbook for the curriculum. This book, *The Journey of GrandPARENT Alienation and Estrangement* was written for the purpose of providing a resource for other estranged parents and grandparents to read and then form faith-based suppport groups in their own localities. Carolyn enjoys gardening, spending time in nature, and volunteering.

www.ingramcontent.com/pod-product-compliance
Ingram Content Group UK Ltd.
Pitfield, Milton Keynes, MK11 3LW, UK
UKHW041842141224
452457UK00012B/597